RESISTANCE FREE
TRAINING

The Basic Ingredients:
Off to a Good Start

by

RICHARD SHRAKE

Foreword by Carol Harris

Trafalgar Square Publishing
North Pomfret, Vermont

First published in 2000 by
Trafalgar Square Publishing
North Pomfret, Vermont 05053

Printed in Hong Kong

Photographs by Jim Bortvedt, except for page 123, which is courtesy of Miller Harness
Company.

Disclaimer of Liability:
The author and publisher shall have neither liability nor responsibility to any person or
entity with respect to any loss or damage caused or alleged to be caused directly or
indirectly by the information contained in this book. While the book is as accurate as
the author can make it, there may be errors, omissions, and inaccuracies.

Library of Congress Cataloging-in-Publication Data

Shrake, Richard.
      Resistance Free training : the basic ingredients / by Richard Shrake.
      p. cm.
ISBN 1-57076-169-8 (hardcover)
    Horses—Training. 2. Horsemen and horsewomen—Training of. I. Title.

SF287.S48 2000
636.1'0835—dc21   00-032550

Cover and book design by Carrie Fradkin
Typeface: Rotis Serif, Rotis Sans Serif
Color separation by Tenon & Polert Color Scanning Ltd

10 9 8 7 6 5 4 3

To my son, Justin...
The Best of the Best

TABLE OF CONTENTS

ACKNOWLEDGEMENTS

First and foremost, I want to thank all of the horse people who have made Resistance Free™ Training the mainstay of their training programs. I am blessed to be a man who has been able to spend his life in an industry he loves. Since I was thirteen years old I knew what I wanted to do with my life and set the goals that have brought me to this day in my life. With almost forty years as a professional horseman I have many individuals to thank for sharing their knowledge and experience with me.

The writing of this book has been a great adventure for me and I hope for those who have joined in the ride. My sincere appreciation goes to Justin Shrake, Bobby Boyce, and Sue Keenan for using their riding talents to communicate the message of Resistance Free Training; Jim Bortvedt whose photographic talent, once again proves he is irreplaceable; Matt and Leslie Day of Hooker Creek Ranch for assisting me with the photo session at their beautiful Central Oregon ranch; Pat Ingram, who was on the ground floor and transcribed my tapes into words; Trafalgar Square Publishing for their professionalism and dedication to educating the horse industry with special gratitude to Managing Editor, Martha Cook and Publisher, Caroline Robbins, who both went above and beyond to see this book through to the finish line; Sue Ducharme, as Collaborator, was invaluable to me, as she took my written words, thoughts, and ideas and presented it in written form for all to understand; Carol Harris, my beloved friend and fellow professional, for her kind words that you will read in the foreword to this book.

Most of all, to my son, Justin, who has shown me through living his life, what life is really all about.

My hat is off to all of you...

May you always ride a good horse!

Richard Shrake

Richard Shrake is a man with unsinkable ideals and ideas who I have known for close to 40 years. I've watched him show horses, judge horse shows, give clinics, hustle business deals, and talk to countless friends. I don't remember ever seeing him upset with anybody, which to me is amazing! Richard is always in control with his easy approach to everything and everyone. The world of horse shows is not always fun. It can be a lonely place, especially for newcomers. Exhibitors are not always warm and gracious to each other, and judges often seem to be cast from the same mold. But Richard is different, and once you have met him with his twinkling eyes, huge smile, and warm hand-shake, you immediately say to yourself "I think this guy really likes me!" To me this is a rare virtue in any person.

During the past 20 years while being involved with Rugged Lark's training, I followed Richard's Resistance Free program with interest because it seemed so similar to the approach we were taking ourselves. Rugged Lark's success speaks for itself, but there is no way we could have done it without using the same kind and compassionate methods that Richard uses in Resistance Free Training.

As I read this book I couldn't help but find deep appreciation for Richard's research and discovery. He has found many areas of interest for you to sink your teeth into and no matter how you interpret his words, you can't help but under-stand horses more completely. He has done a masterful job in taking you on a beautiful journey with a horse of your choice.

I don't believe he is going to make you an instant horse trainer—your dedica-tion, timing, comprehension, and God-given ability must all be in sync for this to happen—but I know that it will be easier for you to achieve success in many puzzling areas that have been a problem in the past. Read these chapters care-fully and think about what Richard is saying. For instance, "Don't hurry anything because horses don't like to be hurried. Remember, they don't wear watches and they don't think we should wear them either." Enjoy Richard's method of organizing his sequence of lessons. Don't take shortcuts or skip around the book because he strongly emphasizes that one lesson is dependent on having learned another.

Most of all remember that Richard Shrake put a lot of time and energy into creating Resistance Free Training so everyone can use and enjoy horses in a manner that does not involve intimidation or cruelty. Sadly, I feel that many horse trainers today do not even like horses. To them horses are merely tools for their trade. This book was written by a man who loves horses. He wrote it for all of us—for beginners, intermediates, and accomplished horsemen—with the sincere belief that no one is ever too old or wise to learn to be kind.

Carol A. Harris

Longtime breeder of champion halter, performance, and racing Quarter Horses, including two-time Superhorse Rugged Lark. She has been an approved judge for The American Quarter Horse Association, The National Reining Horse Association, The National Cutting Horse Association, The American Horse Shows Association, and the American Kennel Club. She breeds and raises world-class Quarter Horses, Thoroughbreds, Whippets, and Italian Greyhounds on Bo-Bett Farm in Reddick, Florida.

A Note to the Reader

The author has provided a glossary for his readers. The words defined in the glossary appear throughout the book in **boldface** type as an indication that the definitions of these terms may be referred to on page 185.

Welcome to the world of RESISTANCE FREE training. I hope that this book will serve as a reliable road map for every trainer—amateur and professional—as you establish a destination and chart your progress in RESISTANCE FREE training with your horses. It's very important to set realistic goals when training horses, just as elsewhere in your life. This book is going to help you set and meet your goals based on the time-proven insights and methods I'll share with you. It will provide consistent benchmarks for evaluating your work. If reaching 100 percent of your horse's potential is a high priority for you, then you are reading the right book.

RESISTANCE FREE training has a proven track record. It's not only a kinder, gentler way of developing a partnership with your horse, but it offers a system of training that makes sure your horse does not have to carry the baggage of abuse, whether mental or physical, along his journey toward becoming a performance horse. RESISTANCE FREE training is based on the **"red and green lights"** of your horse's language: when you understand how to interpret and respond to your horse's signals, you'll acquire an insurance policy against unintentionally putting him in harm's way. You will then find "reading" your horse as practical and simple as watching a thermometer gauge. When your horse is ready to learn and accept training, the gauge will be in the safe "green-light" zone. Training that takes place under these conditions gives your horse the confidence and trust necessary for progress. If you see the "red lights" of resistance, the temperature is starting to soar. Retreat and back off until the temperature drops and the "green light" comes on again.

Using this book, you'll be able to evaluate your horse's progress and adjust your work and your expectations accordingly for your horse on any given day. RESISTANCE FREE training is based on the belief that willing cooperation, positive reinforcement, body language, timing, and **rhythm** are key ingredients that build the kind of partnership between horse and rider you've always dreamed of.

Everyone has to have a destination. When you get on a plane, you know where you're going. It should be the same when you get on your horse. Your destination may change as you travel, but it's important not to just climb aboard and wander at random. This book will keep you traveling on a track of progress through the training maze, instead of detouring into unproductive work.

As a learning process, trial and error is both inefficient and wasteful. It wastes both your time and the performance time of your horse. Every time you go down the wrong path in the training maze, you have to retrace your steps and make the appropriate adjustments in your work just to get back to where you went wrong. The end result is that it will take longer—maybe years longer—to make your horse the best he can be.

In addition, using your horse as an experiment is not good for his mental or physical development. He will lose his generosity and inclination to be a hard worker if he feels as though he gets punished for your lack of experience. You'll save one another a lot of grief if you know the "hows" and "whys" of getting where you want to go.

And this book is full of the "hows" and "whys." You'll find step-by-step guidance in the basics of training your horse, whether he's new to the idea of work, or is already under saddle and could use a refresher course. Part One, *The Heart of* RESISTANCE FREE *Training,* looks at communication between horse and human, the principles of teaching so your horse can learn, and lessons on using your body language as a training tool. I ask you to think about your assets and liabilities as a trainer and offer ideas for strengthening your assets and reducing your liabilities. And then we put those ideas into practice.

In Part Two, I share what I've learned over the years with you in a lesson-by-lesson approach to what I call the Four Phases of your horse's basic training. With these Four Phases, you learn how to get a young horse started correctly for a lifetime of consistent results. And, if your goal is to improve an older horse, use the exercises that begin in Phase One to reprogram him with positive, RESISTANCE FREE techniques. Reschooling your horse in the lessons presented in each phase encourages his cooperation and participation, while rebalancing him in body and mind. By the end of Phase Four, your horse, whatever his age or previous training, will have accepted you as his partner. You will have established a firm but friendly pecking order with you at the top, worked through the important ground exercises that prepare his body and mind, and given your horse a terrific foundation under saddle.

Part Three will offer some insights and solutions for improving "challenging" horses, because I believe that with patience, knowledge, and the right RESISTANCE FREE tools, any horse can be improved. If you're around horses long enough, odds are that some day you'll be faced with a horse who could use some retraining. Perhaps you own one right now.

Once you've mastered the basic ingredients of RESISTANCE FREE training offered in this book, and added some polish and experience, you and your horse will be able to make it to the top of whatever mountain you want to climb together, be it as trail buddies or top-notch competitors.

This book fulfills my lifelong ambition to offer RESISTANCE FREE training as a guide to serve many generations of horsemen and horsewomen. Your grandchildren will find it as beneficial as you do. A hundred years from now, this information will still apply because horses and people will still be fundamentally the same. The sports they participate in may change and so may the trappings, but chances are there will always be situations where a horse and his human won't see things eye to eye. I pride myself on offering timeless insights that will keep riders from getting into trouble with their horses now and in the future. This information won't go out of date next year or next century. It's not tied to the latest trends, fashions, or fads. It's based on enduring principles gathered over a lifetime with horses and their people.

Over the years, I have learned a great deal from my own experiences and from the many trainers I have had the privilege of working with, as well as the many people I have had the pleasure of teaching in seminars. Everyone has contributed something, whether a method, a technique, or simply a better way to explain a relevant point. You can't stop learning. If you do, you become stagnant and out-of-date.

People complain that they don't like change. Well, change is what makes life interesting. I know more this year than I did last year, and next year I'll know even more. The process is ongoing, and appreciating that process makes me a better teacher and trainer—and a better person. It makes it fun for me to sit down and write this book to pass that knowledge on, far into the future.

There are so many people out there in need of guidance and help with their horses. I've done my best to reach as many riders as possible through books, videos, and seminars worldwide because I know from experience that if they don't get that help, they won't meet their own expectations and goals. The answers don't magically appear out of thin air. Thanks to the wide variety of horses and students that I have worked with, I have documented case after case that show Resistance Free techniques work, and work well. That's why I find it so exciting to share them with you through this book.

HOW I LEARNED TO LEARN

When I was young, making the decision to show at the national level was a significant factor in affecting how I would grow as a horseman. I could have stayed at home and showed locally with great success, but I would never have gained that important exposure to the wide range of techniques and methods possible at the national level. Putting myself up against the best helped me hone my abilities to their peak. It doesn't take a "rocket scientist" to realize that you have to have talent and skill to be successful, and being able to learn from those people at the top has been a bonus.

The people who have taken the time to help me along the way have blessed me throughout my life. From my beginnings as a young rider and showman to the present day, I've had the privilege of learning from all types of trainers and horsemen, not just Western-riding trainers. While at competitions with many of these top trainers, I frequently watched them while they schooled their horses (sometimes at three a.m!)

and asked questions about what they were doing and why. I saw their horses change over time. I also observed horses that weren't successful. They were as important in my education as the champions were.

It was clear what worked and what didn't. Realizing the difference helped me develop my long-term goal of being able to help riders and horses at all levels work to the best of their abilities. Year after year, the foundations of those ideas kept building and building into the system of Resistance Free training that I'm presenting to you in this book.

At age twenty-eight, I was asked to do a seminar on Resistance Free training at the Quarter Horse Congress in Ohio, and I found myself lecturing to top horsemen as well as those new to the sport. The feedback I gained from the interesting questions asked by the top hands gave me further insight into what horsemanship was all about. If I had attended the Congress only as a competitor or observer, I could never have derived the benefits I gained as a lecturer, because it put me in a position to pick other people's brains. That proved to be a pivotal point in my development. Resistance Free training gave me a means for sharing a vast amount of knowledge that would have never come to me if I had stayed right at home in Oregon.

Later, being able to attend seminars and shows in many difference countries including Asia and Australia, gave me a more cosmopolitan view of riding as a whole, rather than as a narrow specialization in Western or English riding. It gave me the chance to sit down and really talk with horsemen all over the world. After all, when horse people shoot the breeze, they aren't going to talk about boats, the interest rate, or politics. They talk about horses. I'm grateful for every opportunity to talk horses with people of all levels and sports. I've found that it all fits together in the big picture of horsemanship.

And my judging experience has also shown me lots of different methods, from Colorado cowboy to California vaquero to hunt seat riders and jumpers. Judges see a wide range of talent in the ring. I've judged horses that weren't all that talented or athletic, but because of their schooling and training could outdo horses that were of better quality but had been trained by cruder methods. And while it may sometimes be true that good horses can make good riders, it's far more common to see the opposite effect—a good horse dragged down by an inadequate rider.

Another important factor in my development was the "black and white background" I had while growing up. On the ranch in Salem, Oregon I saw horses come in that had literally been broken in their training. Their will and their spirit was totally gone. I saw horses that had suffered. Wild horses and all kinds of problem horses came down our driveway all the time. I realized then that the old-fashioned technique of restraint—tie 'em up, throw 'em down—wasn't how I wanted to train horses. Number one, it didn't take long to find out that when you restrain a horse long enough to quench his spirit and willingness, it closes many doors later on. All of those horses that had been broken with the use of spirit-breaking Running W's, or hobbled and tied down, were next to impossible to school later in higher movements. Sure, you could ride them—you could get from A to B—but you couldn't get any refinement. A crude beginning made for a crude result.

I also got to visit other facilities that trained expensive weanlings and fine show stock. Those half-million dollar colts were never tied down and subdued until they surrendered. I learned there was another way to get from A to B and on to Z. Perhaps an individual horse was less talented physically, but because he was never hurt in his initial training, his spirit was intact, and he was later able to progress to the top. Instead of dead ends, gentle methods provided unlimited opportunities and a host of open doors for the future. This contrast was a real revelation for me.

Those of us who love horses want to see them go as far as they can. I've worked with everything from ex-racehorses to burnt-out show horses, spoiled backyard stock to horses who were handicapped by their conformation or disposition. Whether rejuvenating an older, working horse or developing a young one, there's a world of knowledge in each situation. I haven't limited my learning and teaching to one breed, either. I've worked with Quarter Horses, Arabians, Morgans, Thoroughbreds, and many more breeds on every level. I've also diversified my sport, not limiting myself to reining or pleasure or cutting. It's my pleasure now to share some of the lessons these many horses and various disciplines have taught me over the years.

Over the past decade I have worked with thousands of horses and riders. Every time that RESISTANCE FREE training works, confidence builds for everyone involved. There were times early on when RESISTANCE FREE techniques didn't work for some people, and I learned from those experiences as well. That feedback allowed me to further my search for techniques that would consistently work for most people. Over the years, I've made refinements that enhanced the training and learning experiences for both horses and their people.

RESISTANCE FREE techniques have been successfully implemented by amateur horsemen, as well as professionals. You and your horse can benefit, too, whatever your background. If you follow the steps to come, you will see some impressive results. The horse you now have may be the most important horse of your life. He may be your dream, he may be your future, or he may be your closest companion. Whatever he is, I want to help your partnership with your horse be the best it can be—RESISTANCE FREE.

A trainer will leave his imprint
on the horses he trains for the rest
of their lives, for better or for worse.
Our goal is "for better."

PART 1

The Heart of
RESISTANCE FREE

Part One of this book will focus on the foundations that support success with RESISTANCE FREE training. I'll start with the basics of horse and human communication, including trust, leadership, and body language. Next, I'll look at the characteristics of a good trainer and how you can develop these qualities. Choosing the right horse as a training partner is key. I'll help you evaluate prospects or assess the horse you already have both physically and mentally and give you some guidelines for setting training and performance goals. Once you've selected the right horse, Chapter Three will take you through the process of preparing your training facilities and handling your prospect to get him ready for the training journey waiting for you in Part Two.

Principles of
RESISTANCE FREE Training

Horses are fun. Sometimes we get away from that, getting too wound up in competition. The horse really doesn't care about that. What the horse cares about is his own well-being and the development of a good relationship with the people that work with him.

Every horse has a slightly different disposition and degree of athletic ability, just as every rider does. My goal is to be able to develop the full potential of both horse and rider, instead of settling for 50 or 60 percent...or less. In this chapter, I'm going to look at the methods that make RESISTANCE FREE training a solid, reliable foundation for your horse, whatever your eventual goals for him. One of the key factors is making sure that your horse willingly accepts his role as a partner in the training process. You can't train effectively—that is, successfully—without his cooperation.

My wide-ranging professional background enables me to eliminate a lot of training techniques and "tricks" that don't work out in the long run. As I said in the introduction, I've worked with many different breeds of horses that have educated me so that I've been able to teach horsemen from all over the world,

some of whom have gained success at national and international levels using my methods. However, it's just as important to me to teach riders who are interested in showing at the local level or the county fair, or who simply want to ride for pleasure—perhaps out on the trails or in the ring—on a good horse. Helping people at all levels develop that good horse is what this book is about.

Humans are taught to do things from childhood. We learn to walk, tie our shoes, use a spoon, read, and so forth. Training a horse—that is, teaching him the basic rules and lessons he needs to lead a successful life as a performance horse—should be a similar process. My hope is that this book will teach you how to educate your horse patiently, at the right speed, with kindness, much as I hope you were taught to do the everyday things in life.

The Four Phases of Training you'll find outlined in this book provide the basic ingredients for preparing the horse to work with you in a spirit of willing cooperation on the ground and under saddle. We're going to focus on getting the core foundation established the right way so that you and your horse will achieve success in the critical early period of your horse's education. The horse's mind is like a computer—

RESISTANCE FREE
TERMS

Bubble: This term refers to a horse's personal space. He's often protective of this area, which could be his entire stall, or a particular part of his body such as his ears, or belly. Horses respond differently to intrusions into their "bubble." While some horses welcome your company, others may respond by saying, "Go away." Become aware of how your horse feels about sharing his space so you can keep him comfortable and focused on learning.

Patterning is an idea I came up with about ten years ago. It consists of turning a negative into a positive. For example, if I'm going to get a horse used to a saddle blanket, I approach the horse with the blanket keeping my eyes down and assuming a non-threatening posture. As soon as the horse begins to show me "red lights"—resistance or panic—I stop, turn my back, and walk away. After a moment or two, I walk back up to him. I may get a foot closer before he begins to show me "red lights" again. Eventually he accepts the blanket and bonds with it. Patterning proves to the horse that he can trust you to work within his comfort zone and keep him from harm.

The **Pizza Theory** is a training approach where the handler introduces new concepts in small steps that are easy for the horse to "swallow." Break each problem, or new idea, into small, comfortable "bites" and teach them one at a time. The smaller steps will be accepted by the horse one by one until the new concept is "old hat."

Preparatory Commands are advanced notices to the horse that a new movement is coming up, either in groundwork or under saddle. They are the yellow traffic lights that let you know that soon you'll have to adjust to another traffic pattern. Imagine the chaos on the roads if green traffic lights turned red without notice! In a similar way, the handler or rider communicates through body language that it's time for the horse to prepare for a movement. The resulting **transition** is more likely to be smooth and satisfying. Effective advance communication like this avoids inadvertent jerks or other abuse that can damage trust and performance.

Red Lights and **Green Lights:** These are important messages from your horse. "Red lights" indicate resistance. They may look like confusion, tension, disobedience, or panic. Sometimes resistance looks like shutting down: the horse just tunes you out as if you were invisible. "Green lights" are the go-ahead signs that indicate that learning is possible. When the horse drops his head, licks and chews, takes a breath, yawns, and is otherwise relaxed and interested, his mind and heart are receptive to you and the lessons you present. The horse can't learn unless his green lights are glowing.

Security Deposits: I often compare using positive reinforcement and the other RESISTANCE FREE training principles to making deposits into a training "bank account." If you make more security deposits— soothing rubs on the withers, or timely uses of the **Pizza Theory**, for instance—than withdrawals—such as meeting resistance with resistance or, worse, temper—your account stays in the black. Keep this account "in the black" with regular investments of positive reinforcement. The result will be a secure and confident horse.

what you put in is what you'll get out. In addition, if you resort to crude methods, you'll be closing "doors" that may never open again. A mistake can snowball into a larger problem that may haunt a horse for the rest of his life. Perhaps you've seen a horse in training that responded by shutting down, closing the doors of opportunity. My drills and exercises are aimed at keeping those doors open. We want to maximize the possibilities, not limit them.

If you fail with a horse, you can get rid of him, but he will have to suffer the consequences of your actions until he is reschooled correctly, or maybe until the end of his days. Training a horse is like an abbreviated process of raising a child. Fortunately it doesn't take as long to train a horse as it does to raise a child, but in the end, we want the same result for both—we want to see that child and that horse go out and do the best possible.

The following principles of RESISTANCE FREE training will build confidence and trust between you and your horse. First, I'll tell you about my philosophy and then help you apply these ideas as you take your horse step-by-step through these Four Phases of Training.

Here's an overview of some training concepts that will become familiar as you continue through this book. I'll discuss each of them in more depth later on and teach you how to use them to make the most of the time you spend training your horse.

UNDERSTAND HOW TO USE RESISTANCE TO BUILD TRUST

Because the horse has emotion and spirit, horse sports are different from "tool" sports like golf, tennis, or boating. The horse can never be parked in the garage or stuffed in the closet when the sport is done. Instead he must be cared for on a constant basis, giving you daily opportunities to create bonds that are not even possible in other sports. Do your golf clubs greet you when you open the closet? Does your boat try to do better every time you go aboard? Building bonds of trust make horse sports unique.

RESISTANCE FREE training provides you with a variety of tools to open the doors to your horse's mental and athletic potential. If I had to pick the most powerful RESISTANCE FREE tool, I'd choose trust. All RESISTANCE FREE training is based on your horse's free choice to participate, which he does because he trusts you. You'll find his level of cooperation is going to relate directly to how much you understand about resistance: what it is—and what it isn't—and how you can transform it into cooperation.

What is resistance? Basically, resistance is your horse's only way to tell you that something you're doing isn't working. He tells you this with his body when he doesn't give you the response that you asked for. In the next section—*Turn Red Lights to Green*—I'll go into how the horse expresses resistance. For now, I want to explain the "why" before the "how." Resistance is instinctive. It's a built-in protective mechanism, and it's his only strategy for coping with mental or physical overload. As we'll see in more detail later on in the section on the **pecking order**, horses were programmed to go with the flow. When your horse gets jammed up, he needs your understanding the most. Resistance is the message he sends with his body that something in your training isn't working.

Turning negatives into positives is a basic RESISTANCE FREE philosophy. If you make a request and your horse says, "No," your horse has just sent you a message. How you decode that message and respond to it can change that "No" to "Yes!" The wrong response can contribute to a spiral of frustration. To help you consistently avoid frustration, let me explain what resistance *isn't*.

Resistance isn't the result of a decision your horse made, because horses don't reason. Resistance isn't a personal insult. Resistance isn't a power struggle, and you can't push the

1 Unlock closed doors and remove the hobbles of resistance by always giving your horse a free choice to be a partner in training.

2 Replace the hours of training time often lost to resistance and trial and error. Instead, make a plan based on knowledge, stay within the horse's comfort zone, and take advantage of the horse's maximum learning curve.

3 Use simple steps of progression. Back up to build confidence and go forward to reach new goals based on trust and lessons already learned.

4 Learn to listen to your horse by watching the "temperature gauge" his "red and green lights" provide. These clues will tell you when the window of opportunity is open and he is ready to learn. If you use force and meet resistance with resistance, you diminish your horse's potential.

5 Use the natural pecking order to earn your horse's trust and build his confidence in you as the trainer and leader.

horse through it. Keeping your horse interested and involved through leadership, softness, and consistency in training is your most important job as a trainer. A horse can't learn if he's busy preparing for battle or flight, which is what resistance is. It's that simple.

Ideally, you could always train within the horse's comfort zone (and this book will give you many strategies for recognizing that zone where maximum learning is possible) and avoid resistance altogether. But this is the real world. At some point in your training program, odds are that your horse will find himself outside his comfort zone. And he'll respond by saying, "No."

The typical horse has the attention span of a three-year-old child. That's pretty short. Maybe his "No" means he needs more time to process right now. Maybe it means "Hey, that *hurts*." Maybe he's like a tired first grader who bursts into tears in the middle of a math lesson because he just can't understand how five and two add up to seven. Resistance means it's time to regroup, to back off—to turn the heat down, not up. You might need to take the lesson back a step or two until you are once again firmly in the horse's comfort zone. Then you can ask him to do something you both know he can do, allowing you to end work for the day on a positive note. If he just doesn't get the idea of five plus two, go back to three plus two and watch the resistance melt away into obedience. And then tell him "Good job."

I'll say it again, because I really want this point to stick with you: resistance is a very valuable training message from your horse. It's your job to listen to the information he's providing, to learn from it, and respond in a way that builds trust. If you get stuck reading resistance as disobedience, you miss the point —especially if you respond with anger or an "I'll teach YOU" attitude. Many of us were taught that if the horse "got away" with any level of disobedience, he would lose respect for us and never cooperate again. The message was that we'd better make him do what we told him, or else. If that took force, well, the horse would respect us for it.

Well, I have a different idea about that. Punishment is never the correct response to resistance. You can't *make* an animal who outweighs you by 800 or 1000 pounds do anything. He has to choose to go along with you. If your horse has just said "No," you can best change that to "Yes!" by understanding that his "No" was not a personal insult directed at you. Remember, horses don't reason. They don't hold grudges. They DO remember abuse and seek to protect themselves from a repetition of that bad experience, but they don't spend hours plotting to make their owners' lives difficult.

As I continue through Chapter One, I'll explore how to use positive reinforcement to transform resistance into softness and cooperation. And finally, I'll look at how your leadership can set the training stage so your horse accepts and respects your role as the boss horse. When you combine kind leadership with positive reinforcement, add a true understanding of the horse's needs and motivations, and develop the ability to adapt your training goals based on the signals he sends you, you'll be able to keep resistance to a minimum. When you do encounter it, you'll know what to do.

Remember, when you adapt to the horse's needs, you haven't given in—you've reassured him that you understand his problem. When he trusts that you're listening and have his best interests at heart, your horse will give you the relaxed "green lights" every horseman wants to see.

Here's a helpful way to look at how to respond to resistance. If you've just noticed that you buttoned your shirt up so you've got more buttons left than holes, do you keep buttoning? Or do you undo them and start buttoning over again? I'll bet it makes more sense to go back and begin again. When your horse says, "Hey, this isn't working," don't keep buttoning!

TURN "RED LIGHTS TO GREEN"

Good trainers are interested in, and open to, the messages a horse sends. This awareness is an important first step in the process of building trust because it reassures the horse that we have his best interests at heart. The horse will never talk back in words, but he will express himself in behavior and rapport. He will give you everything he has and take pleasure in his ability when you know how to interpret and respond to his messages. Horses know when they do well. They also know when you have asked too much. Learn to "listen" to your horse's body language—it will tell you when you are on the right track and when you need to adapt to regain and keep his trust. I call this system of communication between horse and human the "red-light green-light" approach.

With horses, everything begins with leadership. In a herd, horses quickly sort out whose job it is to be boss. There's only one boss, and the rest of the herd follows his or her lead. Their job is to be obedient. Obedience is built-in and natural to horses because without it, they probably wouldn't survive long. (I'll look more closely at the important role of herd dynamics in the section on establishing yourself at the top of the pecking order that fol-

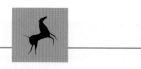

GAINING TRUST

In the early '90s, I was in an arena with a mustang in front of thousands of people at the Reno Wild Horse Expo. I had promised that within an hour, I would be able to touch this little horse who had never been touched before. Well, the clock was ticking. After forty-five minutes, I still hadn't gained the trust I needed to be able to get this horse to allow me to handle him.

I could feel the frustration build. And so could that mustang! He stayed well away from me, testing my trustworthiness big time. Finally, I said to myself, "Richard, time to get quiet." Sometimes under pressure, it's challenging to practice what you preach! So I took a deep breath, dropped down in a squat, and waited. Sure enough, that mustang read my emotional change for the better and he took a step my way. And another. And then he sniffed the hand I offered him. He let me rub him on the shoulder and rewarded me for calming myself down with a dropped head and a big sigh. It's a lesson I've never forgotten. Be trustworthy and horses will trust you.

lows.) The fact is that your horse prefers cooperation to resistance. It's how he was programmed. To gain and keep his trust, it's your first priority as a RESISTANCE FREE trainer to set up his training to take advantage of his instinctive desire to be obedient.

Watch your horse. He will tell you when the window of obedience is open through the body language I call **red and green lights**. Just like a traffic signal, green means go ahead with your training, and red means STOP—right now. When he flashes red lights—pinned ears, a wringing tail, raised head, lips pulled back, stomping feet, maybe a kick or rear—it means his self-preservation instincts are taking over. He's getting ready to "leave town" or do battle. Those reflexes will speed up his heart rate and send blood to his muscles in preparation for action. You've taken your horse too far out of his comfort zone, whether you meant to or not, and he feels threatened. He can't learn when the light is red and you won't be able to just push him through it, either.

Getting back to the green lights—relaxed ears, soft eyes, lowered head, licking and chewing—is your only priority when red-light resistance appears. Any sign of relaxation is a green light and a reliable clue that the fight-or-flight reflexes that are built into his survival instincts are dormant. When he relaxes and his head drops, the blood he requires for clear thinking returns to his brain. Licking and chewing, sighing or yawning are among the actions that release the horse from flight instincts and bring him back into the learning zone (fig. 1.1).

So, to repeat, the first thing to do when the red lights come on and your horse says "No" is to back off. That simple. There shouldn't be any ego at stake. Remember, resistance isn't personal, it's instinctive. It's built in. Once resistance appears, transform it into cooperative RESISTANCE FREE training, there's no schedule more important than whatever it takes to get this right, right now. So if your horse says "No," it's time to get flexible. Think, "Oh, that's interesting," take a deep breath, and give him some quiet space to get his confidence back. Try making yourself smaller—sit or squat down, if it's safe to do so—to remove any perceived threat. Walking a few steps away—again, if it's safe to do so—to remove the pressure is another option. Remember to breathe. In the next section, *Positive Rein-*

1.1 This horse is giving a "green light." He has lowered, and turned his head toward the handler.

forcement, you'll learn some other reliable ways to encourage green lights and also to say "thank you" when they come back on. And always stay calm, because a horse can tune in to your emotions like a mind-reader.

Once your horse has responded to your quiet attitude, look for him to drop his head and relax. He's ready to get back to obedience. When you allow him to work through his resistance quietly, you reassure him that he can trust you. Remember, he's not challenging your authority. When you give him some space, he doesn't respond by getting deeper into your face or your space. He quiets down, thinks it over, and takes a deep breath. The green lights come on. That's how he shows his confidence that you'll be a fair and reliable leader and that he is ready to follow you again.

Your best bet for success once you've got green lights is to take a step back in whatever lesson you were working on. Start the lesson over at a place that's familiar so you set him up for success. Maybe the next time you reach the place that caused him to resist, he'll sail right by. Maybe not. If not, you know what to do. When he does make it past this training plateau, use positive reinforcement to convey your appreciation for the effort.

If you want your horse to trust you, be trustworthy.

POSITIVE REINFORCEMENT

As we've seen, RESISTANCE FREE training is a non-forceful program based on both under-

1.2 Rub this spot right in front of the withers in the direction that his hair grows. This action releases a horse's endorphins, which relax him thus helping the trainer create a bond and build trust.

standing and using the horse's natural instincts and responses to further his education toward partnership as your saddle horse. You will see that when you take responsibility for providing leadership and confidence, your horse will try his best for you of his own free will. Use positive reinforcement to relax your horse and transform red lights to green. Positive reinforcement also tells your horse that you recognize and appreciate his efforts. In essence, you respond to his generosity with generosity of your own. This win-win situation will deepen the bond you seek with your horse and keep those green lights glowing.

There are lots of ways to show your appreciation when your horse tries hard for you. The method you choose isn't as important as the fact of doing it. People have all kinds of opinions on this issue. One I hear all the time is, "But Richard, he'll get spoiled!" I hear people

say that about kids, too, but a good kid who gets recognized for doing good work appreciates being appreciated and shows it. Same with horses, or dogs, or just about any other domestic creature. Positive reinforcement generally improves confidence and pride in accomplishment, as well as the desire to keep doing good work that gets recognized and rewarded. Have you ever worked for an appreciative boss? What about a boss who spoke only to reprimand you? Which boss would you go the extra mile for? I rest my case.

One approach I use time and time again to reward the horse and build trust at the same time is to rub in front of his withers in a circle in the direction the hair grows (fig. 1.2). You can reach this spot from his back or the ground. Rubbing the soft spot on the dock of his tail also works (fig. 1.3). These are areas where mares nuzzle their foals. Stimulating

1.3 Another place to release endorphins is the top of the dock where a mare often nuzzles her foal.

these areas releases endorphins, the body's own relaxing chemicals. Most horses quickly drop their heads and get a soft expression in their eyes in response. There are several other soothing spots: along his poll, jowls, gums, and ears, as illustrated (figs. 1.4 to 1.8). When you make use of these calming and pleasurable triggers that Nature provided, your reassurance and "thank you" come through loud and clear. You are communicating in positive language that the horse is programmed to understand immediately.

Your voice can also be a powerful reward. Horses do respond to some human language, but your tone of voice is more important than your words. If you sound positive—enthusiastic or quietly pleased—your horse knows from your tone that he's done well. Likewise, look out if you find your voice getting angry or cold. The horse is liable to shut you out or

respond aggressively to the perceived threat. If you get forceful, you trigger instinctive, self-protective behaviors in him. If he has to protect himself from you, he can't focus on learning, for one thing. For another, there goes the trust you've been building. You can rebuild it if you're careful, but it is going to take time away from progress. Just keep quiet, or better yet, walk away for a bit if you feel your own red lights beginning to glow. Use your voice responsibly, positively, and honestly.

This last quality is important. If your praise is not honest, you are going to confuse, or maybe annoy, the horse. He should understand what response you've reinforced him for. Cause and effect—that is, effort and reward—need to be clearly related. Be sure that you reinforce him for honest effort so you don't teach him that reward is cheap. Make positive reinforcement meaningful and in proportion, and watch

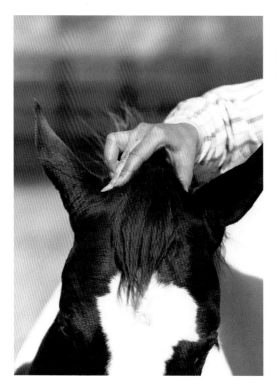

1.4 Light pressure on both sides of the poll relaxes and lowers this horse's head.

1.5 Rub right above his eye, another soothing spot, to release endorphins.

your horse become more quietly confident.

For many sensitive horses, simply removing the pressure in response to a good effort is a reward in itself. For instance, he shifts his hindquarters when you lightly press his side with your calf. When you stop the calf pressure the horse knows you stopped because he did what you asked and is satisfied with his half of the bargain. I think you can add obvious signs of your appreciation without worrying about your horse getting greedy or spoiled. Always observe how your horse reacts to gauge whether you're on the right track or not. If his behavior improves, your message is getting through loud and clear. Otherwise, change your approach.

Here's an idea I refer to often—**Security Deposits.** I often compare positive reinforce-

ment with making deposits in a bank. Each time you provide your horse with positive input—a soothing rub on the shoulder, quiet aids—it's like making a goodwill deposit in his bank. The more security deposits you make, the more secure and confident your horse becomes. Likewise, if you make more withdrawals than deposits, the account goes into the red. RESISTANCE FREE trainers make a conscious effort to keep the balance in the black. To make sure your investment grows, make regular contributions to his well-being with positive reinforcement.

A relaxed, confident horse is what RESISTANCE FREE training is all about. Change resistance to obedience, gain his trust, and your horse becomes a partner you can rely on. In the next section, I'll teach you about establishing your-

1.6 Use the back of your hand like a feather over the tips of his ears to help your horse become "soft."

1.7 Release more endorphins: with your fingers rub the jowls in a circular motion.

self at the head of the pecking order so you create the obedience and mutual respect necessary for RESISTANCE FREE training to work effectively. I'll also provide some insights into horse and human communication that will increase your awareness of what his body is saying to you and yours is saying to him. And as you continue through this book, I'll give you lots of ideas for turning "I can't" into "I can!"

THE PECKING ORDER:
PUT YOURSELF AT THE TOP

The pecking order is how animals and birds sort out a hierarchy within their groups that determines who is in charge and who has dominance over another. There will be a "General," or leader, and there will be a "Private," the one who is at the very bottom of the ranks. Nobody dares pick on the General. He or she gets first pick of the food, makes all the decisions about where to go and when to do it, and can dominate any other animal in the group. The number-two animal can pick on every other except for number one, and so on right down the ranks. The animal at the bottom is always the last to eat and usually looks like a punching bag because everybody is getting a piece of him. The pecking order shifts constantly whenever new animals enter the group and as other animals develop the confidence to challenge those above them. If a challenger defeats an animal above him in status, he is then superior to that individual. He may have to fight a lot of other animals in order to sort out where everybody ranks in relation to him.

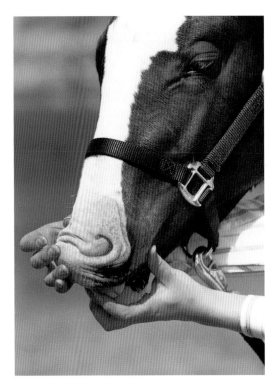

1.8 Rub the gum just above the two front teeth in a circular motion—another calming area that can really relax your horse.

horse will obey you and look to you for instructions. You'll find that your job is ten times easier.

In a group situation, the horse that controls another horse's space by getting him to move out of the way is the horse that moves up a notch in the pecking order. The horse that loses moves to the outside of the herd and the winner steps up in rank. This pattern of a natural behavior sets the horse up for allowing a new superior to emerge from the herd. In this case, you.

All horses really want to be followers, even the Generals, believe it or not. Just watch them in a field. One horse makes the decision about when to eat, drink, and go to the shade. If the leader raises his head and starts to run, everybody joins in. It's part of the herd survival mechanism. The key to setting yourself up as the General is to allow your horse to assume the role of follower (fig. 1.9).

As we've seen, it's a basic instinct for any horse, even the General, to obediently let a more dominant force decide where to go and how fast to get there. It's clearly in your best interest to apply for that job. Basically, you win the position by using your body language to convey your confidence in your abilities to handle the role and to convince the horse you're the candidate he can trust to do the job right. As the trainer, you'll take over the responsibility for making decisions. Remember, he really doesn't want the responsibility himself.

In your role as the leader, dominant doesn't usually mean aggressor, though if you're working with a horse who is the General in his herd, you might need to get pretty assertive at times. It may be a little more challenging to establish yourself as the boss, but it's worth the effort. Be very aware of the sometimes fine line between assertive and threatening. Remember that if he feels threatened, he will respond by challenging you right back. You can't win this battle, so don't go there. Be respectful of his superior strength and use your mind and body to win him over to your corner.

When a racehorse dumps his jockey, he usually catches right back up with the rest of his "herd." Loose horses finish the Grand National Steeplechase in England all the time. People think it's because the horse loves to race and jump, but it's really just natural behavior. These horses shed their riders and return to the herd, often right out in the lead because they aren't handicapped by the weight of a rider. (The jockeys understandably don't like this scenario because a loose horse can change his mind at any second about whether to jump the next obstacle—some horrendous accidents have occurred when the following riders and horses were interfered with by a riderless horse.) However, as a trainer you can use this instinctive inclination to follow the herd to your advantage. After establishing yourself as leader, the

1.9 The pecking order in action—the herd is following the "General" horse.

Body Language Basics

If you ever have the privilege of observing horses in the wild, you'll notice that those who seek to be aggressive and dominate another horse will tighten their bodies and make violent, sudden movements into the other horse's space. If the challenged horse is weaker or more subservient by nature, he will surrender his space and retreat. The dominant horse's actions are the equivalent of shouting an order. The lesser horses respond very quickly to avoid the possible nip or kick that may follow that "order."

In contrast, slow movements draw horses to one another. They welcome one another into shared space instead of seeking to expand their private space. Relaxed, slow steps and body motions express calmness to the others.

Reading a domestic horse's intentions through his body language can be pretty straightforward, especially if you imagine what the message might say to another horse. If a horse raises his head high above you or turns his rump to you, trying to knock you down, he's challenging your right to be there. If you see a clamped-down tail and pinned ears, this horse is expressing his intention to set you firmly beneath himself on the pecking order. The way to change his mind is to take over the role of boss horse and control his space by moving him out of his.

To do this and keep him out of your space, match any quick moves on his part with equally quick moves of your own. What counts is the *ability* to make the first strike, not to actu-

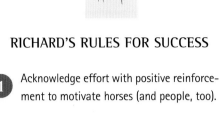

RICHARD'S RULES FOR SUCCESS

 Acknowledge effort with positive reinforcement to motivate horses (and people, too).

 A relaxed horse is ready to learn.

 Communicate kindly with your horse.

 A trainer is totally responsible for training outcomes.

5 You become the leader by humanely controlling the horse's space.

6 A good leader applies pressure within the boundaries of the horse's comfort zone for maximum learning.

7 Avoid senseless repetition. When you've achieved your goal, acknowledge the good work and quit.

8 Set the horse up for success: always allow him to choose to be obedient.

9 Horses' attitudes can be changed with patient training.

10 Resistance is a great training tool. Use the information it provides to make progress.

ally connect. So if you need to establish physical boundaries, a quick snap of your arm or elbow toward his face that stops before connecting makes the point that you could have made contact if you needed to. He will understand that and concede the point, and some respect, to you. Take a deep breath and use your outstretched arms around when you want to move him forward. Remember that your tone of voice conveys powerful messages. If he's aggressive, respond with an aggressive tone. When he drops or turns his head, relaxes his tail, starts to chew, or takes a deep breath, you've got green lights. Green lights tell you in equine body language, "I want to be obedient. I want to listen to you." Really watch for these clues that tell you the horse is in the "follow" mode and ready to accept your leadership. You have then gained a level on the pecking-order totem pole, completely through observing and using body language.

Placing yourself in the role of leader is generally easier with a horse already used to being in the middle of the ranks. When I begin groundwork with him, the in-between horse is pretty open-minded. I start out by teaching him that I'm in charge of his space. As I enter the stall, I take a little time to watch the horse and see how he responds to me. If he walks over, maybe rubs me with his head, or swings his rump in my direction, the horse is challenging my position in the pecking order. I get a halter on as soon as possible to put me in control of his "**bubble.**" Because smelling is a horse's way of saying hello, I offer him the back of my hand—there is far more scent there. Then, I begin to move his shoulders and hips around by pressing my hand against his sides until he shifts away from the pressure. In this way, I use body language to take charge of his movements and become the leader. When he respects me as his leader, it makes it easy for him to take the role of follower. (I'll talk more about controlling his space by shifting various parts of his body in Chapter Four.)

With a horse who is a "Private," his confidence is your goal. So become very nonthreatening. Go low and get small in the stall as he walks around and gets used to your presence. Once he's given you signs of relaxation and acceptance, you can move around him confidently. While you stand or walk near his shoulder, change his direction by quietly lifting your outspread arms to shoulder level. Use your open arms to channel him to the left or right. To signal him to stop his movement, first stop your own motion. Then, from a position forward of his shoulders, turn your whole body, including your feet, so you're facing his withers. Your toes should point toward his shoulders. Soon, you'll find that pointing your toes this way will bring him to a full stop every time. Let him know when he stops moving that this is what you want. Rub his shoulder and use your voice softly. Your reward will be the green lights that tell you this horse has allowed you to go to the head of the pecking order.

In his life as a domestic partner, the horse wants to be able to rely on you as a confident leader. Watching a person lead a horse is a very good guide to how he or she will do as a trainer and "boss horse." For instance, watch as he or she leads the horse off, and resists a little. If the trainer immediately turns around to look at the horse, it reinforces any insecurity the horse has. He gets a confirmation that yes, forward isn't someplace he wants to go. The hesitant, insecure person who always looks back at a horse while leading is actually reinforcing the horse's doubt in that unreliable leader. This behavior looks to him like lack of confidence. The horse will be less inclined to obey and more likely to do whatever the spirit moves him to do if he judges you to be subordinate to himself.

People with positive body language, such as square shoulders and a steady **cadence** to their movement, do well as trainers. Horses perceive such body language as assertive and controlling, and they respond to it favorably. Avoid acting hesitantly or negatively. Displaying direct and straightforward body language should become one of your primary goals as a RESISTANCE FREE trainer.

As you continue your horse's education, groundwork becomes one of the best training tools for controlling his space. After you become the boss, you'll use his natural inclination to follow your lead to teach the horse to keep working until you give him permission to stop. The level of obedience that you need in your chosen sport determines the amount of control you need to establish with your horse. For instance, a reining horse has to allow his rider total control. Therefore, he must be set up to be completely obedient. Groundwork, which relies on body language to relax the horse's mind so he accepts you as the General, really gets *you* into his mind through his body.

RESISTANCE FREE training is rooted deeply in groundwork, as you'll see in Part Two when we begin to work with your horse. One of the primary goals in groundwork is to allow any horse to go into the "follow" mode, as we just achieved in the stall, by moving his shoulders and hips, and controlling his space. Groundwork is invaluable for many reasons, including developing the horse's mental and physical maturity. But using it as a stress-free route to the head of the pecking order may be the most important reason of all to use groundwork as the foundation of your training.

The "Eyes" Have It

How you use your eyes around a horse has a lot to do with whether that horse will trust you or not. Generally, it's wise to avoid direct eye contact; horses will read your stare as a challenge. Some Arabian halter trainers deliberately use direct eye contact to provoke their stallions to "puff up" and respond to the challenge, which gives them a spectacular, aggressive appearance in the ring. Since under most circumstances, we prefer the horse to be calm, not aggressive, be aware of how strongly your eyes can influence your horse's attitude.

How you use your eyes also tells the horse a lot about your intentions, so be sure you use them to convey the right message. "**Hard eyes**" focus narrowly on one thing, often to the exclusion of the surroundings. For example, stare directly at your thumb, so hard that you are not able to focus clearly on anything else. This is a hard, or narrow eye. Now soften your vision, look at the thumb, and include the surrounding area in your peripheral vision. You may not notice as many specific details about your thumb, but you can now absorb general details about the background. "**Soft eyes**" encompass an entire plane, so that your peripheral vision effectively tracks everything that happens around you. Soft eyes are more friendly and welcoming to horses—and people—than a hard stare.

Try it yourself when greeting people you don't know. Scowl and stare at the next person you see with hard eyes and notice the response. They're probably going to be a little apprehensive of you, and may subconsciously acknowledge you as being above them in the pecking order! Use friendly, soft eyes on the next individual, and note the difference in his attitude toward you. Now try it on horses. Remember that you want to be dominant, but you don't want to achieve leadership through a knock-down, drag-out fight. Walking into a stall and confronting a horse with narrow, hard eyes will make him nervous and trigger his desire to escape.

Many successful trainers are masters of indirect eye contact, maintaining control of the horse without ever confronting him with an intimidating eye-to-eye stare. They use their body language to dominate and lead the horse through his work. Horses by their nature seek out these subtle movements and respond to them in a positive manner, taking comfort in being led and controlled because it occurs in a natural manner, through body language instead of clumsy tack. These skillful people use every cell of their body to tell the horse where they are going and why, like a beam of light shining through the darkness, drawing the horse to follow the light by instinct.

There are people who do use direct eye contact, and eventually a horse can learn to accept that confrontational look because he will realize that despite all appearances, he isn't going to be harmed. At first, though, he will be more interested in saving himself from a possible attack than in learning what the trainer has in mind. Avoid this habit yourself.

Horses who are chronically hard to catch will be even more difficult when hard eyes are used. Trainers with short tempers are more likely to focus closely and intently on the problem horse, going "into" hard eyes, and sending out body-language alarm signals to every horse in the field. The result is that a difficult horse becomes even worse. The horse can read that body language with ease, and the more impatient and angry the trainer gets, the more anxious the horse is to avoid capture.

Someday when you aren't in a hurry, try using hard eyes when you go out to catch your horse. He will look at your approach with wariness instead of welcome. If the two of you have formed a solid relationship, the catching will still be no problem, but the horse's whole attitude may do an about-face. Instead of a companionable greeting, you'll receive a colder welcome.

On the other hand, with the spooky horse try moseying out to the field as though you haven't a care in the world and don't really have any idea of doing anything anyway. Neutral body language and soft eyes will often gain you quicker results because you pose no threat.

This goes back to the predator-prey relationship. Zeroed-in eye contact doesn't come any more concentrated than in the hard eyes of a lion stalking a zebra. Other zebras in the herd that are not in the immediate vicinity are totally casual about the whole thing because they know they aren't close enough to risk being noticed by those focused, hard eyes. Grazers of other species will also watch the action with the air of spectators at a football game. On the other hand, if the stalking predator is distracted he will shift to soft eyes to see what is going on around him, and may well lose that particular prey along with his concentration.

Experiment with hard eyes on the animals you meet. Just be careful. Hard eyes aimed at some dogs will get you bitten!

I'll give you another example. The effects of hard eyes versus soft, open eyes apply to riding bicycles as well as riding horses. If you focus on the bicycle tire, you will lose your balance (if you haven't collided with something first). On horseback, if you tend to stare down hard at the horse's neck or ears, instead of looking where you are going with soft eyes, the performance that results will be stiff and tense, which will not display your horse at his best. The lesson here? Soft eyes are valuable tools in the RESISTANCE FREE horseman's collection.

INTRODUCING PREPARATORY COMMANDS

When you're handling the horse on the ground or later under saddle, your body should communicate your requests early, loudly, and clearly. **Preparatory Commands** serve as quiet signals that have a powerful impact on your horse's ability to follow your leadership. Think of Preparatory Commands as advanced notice to the horse that a movement is coming up, the way yellow traffic lights let you know that soon you'll have to adjust to another traffic pattern. Imagine the chaos on the roads if green lights turned red without notice! With Preparatory Commands as an advanced warning, the resulting **transition** or movement is more likely to be smooth and satisfying. Effective communication like this avoids inadvertent jerks or other abuse that can damage trust and performance.

Remember to use the Preparatory Body Commands consistently in your work. For example, let's see how this works when you're teaching a horse how to move and stop on the lead line. Begin by holding the lead in your left hand and keeping your right hand free.

To go forward, the Preparatory Command is to lean forward slightly. When working with a young horse, first you make a very obvious upper body movement. Within a couple of weeks, the movement becomes more and more subtle, and you can eventually do little more than nod your head forward and the horse responds.

When you get ready to stop, raise your right hand before you actually stop and tuck your rear end underneath your body, just as you would to make a swing go higher. This movement gives the horse a yellow light to get ready to stop. At first, follow this with downward pressure on the lead rope for the actual stop, then give the horse a quick, clear release of pressure when he responds appropriately. Later on, when he's clear about how to behave on a lead line, the Preparatory Command for a stop will be to lean back slightly with your upper body.

When you want him to turn, your upper body should turn in that direction before you actually begin the turn. That Preparatory Command and yellow light is what creates your leadership role signaling "follow me" to your horse. A slight turn of the head will eventually be enough. Remember, if the horse can respond to or see a fly, he can certainly notice your slightest movement.

Begin with exaggerated movements at first to give the horse clear signals. Wait for him to learn, and be careful to correct him before he can make any mistakes. Preparatory Commands teach the horse to relax and trust you much more quickly because he can rely on you to make it easy to succeed. Without Preparatory Commands, lessons take eight times as long to teach.

CONSISTENCY MATTERS

If you establish a consistent training program, it may pay off with as much as 20-percent increase in the horse's performance. Under these optimum conditions, he may learn quicker, experience fewer setbacks, and mature ahead of his peers. The young horse will be ready to sell earlier than others in his age group, if that's your goal.

Wild horses lead a very precise, time-oriented existence. They do the same things at the same time everyday unless something interferes. When I was with one of the top wild-horse gatherers in Nevada, he explained to me that a particular band of wild horses would come down the trail and step over a specific rock sometime between 10 A.M. and 10:37 A.M. I was dubious because that was nearly 24 hours away. This range covered 150,000 acres. How could anyone know where those horses would be at any given time? The next day the band came right down the trail at 10:37 A.M., right when and where he said they would.

Domestic horses also lead a time-oriented existence. If you don't agree, just be late with dinner and watch them start to get upset. In college, I helped with an experiment in horse behavior and training. We took ten foals, put them on the same quantity of feed, and fed them religiously at 7 A.M. and 5 P.M., without fail. Another group of ten foals was put on the identical rations but was fed on a random basis. The first group, the scheduled foals, gained 20 percent more growth than the randomly fed group and was much easier to be around. The next month we switched the two groups, altering the scheduled group to random feeding. It was incredible how the two groups changed. The foals that had been fed consistently and growing well got flightier and didn't thrive as well as they had. The foals in the first random group improved when they were fed on a regular basis.

So to get the most out of your work together, especially in the beginning of training, organize your sessions on a regular basis and always include a warm-up. The goal is to set it up so that your horse regularly meets his peak of learning ability at about the same point in each lesson. When he feels secure at that point, you can really move forward in his later work. Don't overstep the logical bounds of what he can handle in one session however, or all of your work goes for nothing. It will take days to recover the horse's original level of acceptance and relaxation if you push him beyond his limits even once.

These boundaries vary from horse to horse. Some horses, usually geldings, will forgive you for occasional mistakes in judgment and not hold them against you. Mares may become fearful in the same situation, and a stallion might have second thoughts about cooperating. In the next chapter, I'll talk more about understanding how to gauge your horse's tolerance for training.

If you don't have patience,
you have no business training horses.

CHAPTER 2

Build the Partnership:
Evaluating Trainer and Trainee

EVALUATE YOUR POTENTIAL AS A TRAINER

Do you have what it takes to be an effective RESISTANCE FREE horse trainer? If you decide to be a doctor, you have to go through a lot of schooling before you're ready to start performing surgery. Getting a driver's license requires education and testing before you are allowed to hit the road solo. Likewise, you need to establish some minimum skills and qualifications before you head for the training pen. To be a RESISTANCE FREE horse trainer, you need a love for horses, understanding of the horse's needs and his language, endless reserves of patience, and a plan for what you want to achieve and how you're going to get there. Most of all, you need to be excited about seeing a horse progress and achieve proficiency in his training.

So many people omit preparation and learning from the horse-training equation, assuming that they'll just instinctively know what to do when the time comes. Parents assume that their child will automatically be able to work with an unbroken two-year-old so that they can show in every class at the county fair—which is two months away! I've seen it all. It doesn't have to

be that way. Be as well prepared to work with your horse as you are for your profession, and your training road will be a lot smoother.

In this chapter, you'll learn how to evaluate and select an appropriate horse to work with. You'll also get tips on evaluating the horse you already have and how to assess his strengths and perhaps his liabilities in light of the goals you have for him. These goals are very important. RESISTANCE FREE training can improve any horse, but if your horse wasn't designed by Nature to be a world-class racer or reiner, you may have to consider a new goal—or a new horse. I'll focus on your role in the training equation, too. Horse training takes a special kind of person. I hope I can help you become the kind of trainer any horse would willingly accept as a partner.

The majority of people who attend the RESISTANCE FREE graduate program have experienced a plateau in their training and see this course as an opportunity to make progress. Most of them have an eventual goal of teaching others, and some participants plan to train horses professionally. To help students better understand whether a career training horses is in their future, I like to have them write down their training goals. I ask them to list as many good things about their horses as they can. Again and again, the ones who turn out to be successful will list several times as many good things as bad things about their horses.

Perhaps we have a student who lists a lot of negatives for his horse and only a few good things. One thing that works well in our program is to have this student concentrate exclusively on the horse's good qualities. Over time, this often creates a totally different picture. If, on the other hand, the student has nothing whatsoever good to say about the horse, not even that he has a nice coat, a good tail, is easy to catch, or whatever, we usually find that there is a locked door there and no key in sight. Some people just don't have what it takes to succeed as a RESISTANCE FREE trainer.

A lot has been written on human personalities and how they relate to horsemanship. I think the positive traits of successful horse people include:

◆ quiet patience

◆ a good command of body language and Preparatory Commands

◆ the ability to plan out their actions ahead of time

◆ a tendency to be a little slow and more deliberate in their actions, rather than jumping quickly from one thing to another

◆ hands that move in sync with their body

◆ coordination among all of their body parts as they move

◆ even temperament: very few quick-tempered people make good horsemen because temper always gets them in trouble

The Resistance Free Training Attitude

A horse trainer with a proper attitude will clearly show that he or she likes horses. Are you excited about working with your horse, so much so that you will be with him everyday? Once you decide to head out on this training journey, set yourself up so you and your horse arrive at your destination together, as partners.

RESISTANCE FREE training takes time and patience. You must be able to develop a rapport and bond with the horse. You can reach realistic goals, but the true pleasure will lie in the training journey, not the destination.

Plan your day before you arrive at the barn and decide what you want to see happen today. Look for the green lights of success. Mentally review the yellow caution lights that indicate areas needing more work, and determine what must be done to keep the red lights of resistance from coming on.

Arrive for each day's sessions with an open mind. Observe the horse as you work together and be alert for the slightest signs of obedience and appreciate them. Don't take your bad day at work out on your horse. If you have to, take a time-out before you go to the barn and tune your mental attitude up to optimistic.

So many trainers do go to the barn lugging yesterday's problems with the horse along with them. Leave these behind. Don't punish the horse today because of the problems he had the day before. Give him a fresh opportunity to learn. Take a slightly different approach that may click. If you run into a problem, break it down into the smallest possible segments and correct it, one segment at a time—what I call the **Pizza Theory.** Take baby steps forward instead of giant steps backward and praise generously for the slightest hint of improvement.

Later, you'll also find that doing some simple groundwork with your horse before getting in the saddle will help get both your minds on track. Whether longeing, practicing leading, or working through an obstacle, this work can help the pair of you focus. This is why I recommend that each of the Four Phases of Training in Part Two include groundwork everyday. The grooming process is also a significant part of your preparation. If you're having a bad day, put some extra time into the grooming. This can work wonders with your attitude.

A RESISTANCE FREE trainer pays close attention to the horse's natural inclinations when planning what direction to take him in. Don't lock yourself into set expectations just because a horse is bred a certain way, or because his mother was a super performer. The horse is an individual, for example, he may not be cut out to be a star in the Working Cowhorse division. Maybe he is better running barrels.

Just because this horse is a strong-willed colt, don't hold it against him for the rest of his life. If he retains some of this attitude, look for an event where a brassy demeanor is a plus, not a minus. He might make a super cutting horse, or a terrific team-penning horse.

A laid-back horse will make his way more easily in the trail classes. There, his calmer attitude is a plus. In the speed events, it might be a minus, but that depends on the individual. Sometimes a well-trained tortoise will outdo a rowdy hare!

If you firmly believe you've chosen a good horse, you're excited about him, and you have the right tools for his training, you have put together the ingredients for success.

Don't let negative experiences with previous horses of a certain bloodline color your expectations—good or bad—of your current horse. Some trainers will remember that "snaky" gelding that couldn't get out of his own way, and consciously or subconsciously assume that all the other horses of that bloodline share that trait. They don't like the horse before they even begin. Don't let that happen to you.

Keep it Positive

Don't let your training program overwhelm you. If your attitude begins to show a little wear and tear, break down your goals into smaller, achievable ones so that you can enjoy some successes, however small. Be pleased with the smallest progress.

We don't start out with the main event; we

MISTAKEN IDENTITY

A few years ago, a Quarter Horse owner dropped off a King Fritz gelding and a Sir Quincy Dan gelding at the barn. I wasn't in at the time. It happened that the King Fritz was a chestnut, and the Quincy Dan, a bay. Tom St. Hillarie was working for me, and he also had a King Fritz gelding named Mr. Power Chex. This was a great horse who had won several top-ten championship youth titles for Tommy, who was definitely a King Fritz fan as a result.

King Fritzes are wonderful cowhorses with great minds. The Quincy Dans are terrific halter horses but never had the best mind as far as quietness, or suppleness. I had Tommy start both colts that summer, and every time I went out to see them, Tommy bragged about that King Fritz gelding. He said it was the smartest thing that ever walked in the gate. He had nothing good to say about the Quincy Dan horse. The Quincy Dan horse didn't make a lot of progress. He kept running into dead end after dead end in his work.

Sixty days later, the owner came to see how his horses were progressing. Tommy got out the little bay and bragged on how, as usual, a King Fritz colt was going to be a world champion. The owner looked puzzled, and when Tommy had finished working both horses, it was pretty obvious that the bay was the A-plus student. The chestnut was pretty mediocre. Then the owner pointed out that the bay horse was the Sir Quincy Dan and the chestnut was the King Fritz, and Tommy nearly fell off the horse!

It goes to show how mental expectations can shape the results of your training.

start out with the tiniest little beginning and improve on it over a period of time. Always make sure that your horse can do it before you ask him to do it. In turn, this keeps your attitude good.

Jimmy Williams, the late, world-renowned Californian hunter and jumper trainer who trained at the Spanish Riding School, always said, "When you're training horses, never let your horse know what it can't do." If you're training the horse and asking him for more than he is ready to do, you're doing just that. Something as simple as moving away from the leg might be more than he is ready to do that day. But if you ask him to move away from your leg by kicking him in the belly, you haven't done your homework in developing this movement. Start from the ground and ask the horse to step away from the pressure of your finger, and you will begin to develop a pattern that will eventually lead to the most sophisticated exercises. When you build up the horse with little successes, he gains confidence.

If the pressure of a finger doesn't do it, you may need to break down the exercise still further and help him along by bringing his head around, causing his body to move in the opposite direction. Teach him to associate that body movement with your finger pressure, and you've accomplished something. After a few days of basic exercises like these, you can get on his back, apply a little pressure, and he will respond because you have installed the button for that response. You both now know he can do it.

The horse is very sensitive during the first Four Phases of Training, and we can make or break him with our attitude. For example, a horse might be hard to catch or have difficulty with groundwork, so we tend to expect problems with future training exercises just because we've had difficulty in those areas. In other words, we've locked the door of the future because we have a negative expectation.

Often, problems arise because you expect too much. In these situations, stop, watch, and wait.

Time is a wonderful thing to have on your side. The old saying goes, "If you give your horse a lesson by mistreatment, you'd better look out because he's liable to learn from the lesson." I've updated this to say, "If you give your horse a lesson with resistance, you'd better look out because he's likely to learn from the lesson." Keep your expectations based on your work together on that day.

A new paved road might look pretty, but if the groundwork wasn't done before the pavement went on, it will soon buckle and develop potholes. Your horse is the same way. He might look pretty for a little while, but the holes will eventually show up. Make sure his foundation is solid.

There will be many plateaus in training where progress slows for a time, and the temptation is to force a horse to progress by coercive methods or aggressive riding. If the horse has a history of abuse in his past—for example, trouble with being clipped or trailered—his progress now will be slower because you have to be especially careful to smooth over those ingrained behavioral responses before you can continue. Plateaus are to be expected. Remember, it takes what it takes. It's up to you to set him up to succeed by keeping him in his comfort zone whenever possible and always keeping an eye open for red lights that you can change to all-clear green lights.

You'll never be able to read your horse unless you allow yourself to have the mental attitude that lets you look for the green lights. Your horse won't progress in an orderly manner. A negative attitude will turn on the red lights that stop progress. So do your best to keep it positive. If you can't, don't train that day.

Ultimately a horse can't progress in his training until we open the doors of opportunity for him.

SPOTTING A GOOD TRAINER
(AND A BAD ONE)

The true horseman is always looking for the good things in the horse. As a result, the horse will produce more and more desirable qualities. The handler or rider who is always looking for flaws, mistakes, and misbehavior is going to create problems instead of correcting them. If your horse has a problem, the first place to look is in the mirror! If you are always blaming the horse, you're in for a tough time as a trainer. If you are willing to go back and examine yourself as a potential source of problems, it keeps the door open. Progress for both horse and human becomes possible.

The guy who is always blaming the "stupid horse" is going to have a barn full of "stupid horses." The one who treats every horse like a champion will find training to be rewarding in progress as well as success. This person stays on track, and there is no limit to what he can accomplish.

Effective individuals know what they're going to accomplish with their horses before they ever get to the barn. They have a plan in mind, and will work on that plan, unless they find some circumstance that changes the plan for them. In that situation, the positive trainer will modify the plan to something that can be achieved that day, under those conditions.

For example, the ineffective trainer might arrive, determined to school flying changes today. Come hell or high water, it's flying-changes day. It doesn't matter whether or not the horse is having a good day himself, or that perhaps the groundwork for changes isn't there, or that there is a lot of chaos at the barn today, or that the arena is a bog.... By gosh, they're still going to do flying changes.

The effective trainer considers what's going on with the horse, what things are like at the barn, and perhaps decides that today would be better spent on a trail ride, or that more work is needed on Preparatory Commands and basic

work instead of advancing to flying changes. If things go very well, that person might do *one* flying change at the end of the training session and immediately put the horse away, ending on a good note.

The other trainer will struggle and jam the horse around, perhaps get a flying change or two, and keep right on working. The horse gets heated-up and nervous, and the rider gets more and more abrupt, until the horse is totally unable to comprehend anything. I'm sure you've seen this scenario again and again, whether it's schooling changes or walking across a bridge on a trail.

To be the effective trainer, always remember: your horse is not an adversary; he's a partner. If you don't keep your half of the bargain, it's unlikely the horse will keep his.

Over the years I've observed that the professional who successfully deals with the training of problem horses is the trainer who cares and forgives and takes a real interest in the horse rather than just looking for a band-aid correction or searching for a button to push.

With young horses, the successful trainer is the guy who keeps his cool under all circumstances. No matter what happens, he sticks with RESISTANCE FREE training. The unsuccessful trainer is the one with the unreliable personality who goes along fine until he reaches a sticking point or loses his temper, and then he creates a wound in the horse's mind that his personality will never allow to heal. That open wound turns a promising prospect into a problem horse that has to be pasted back together before he can go on in his work.

Watch out for trainers whose horses all have the same problem. They're nervous, they're all on edge, and they want to get away. They are always on the muscle and blowing up. From the outside you can see clearly that the trainer is the problem. You never want this kind of "professional" to handle your horse.

Trainers who take every ounce of credit for the work their horses do well aren't successful trainers, in my book. When you talk to one of these guys, it's always "I" this and "I" that. "I put the 'stop' on him and I won the futurity with him." It's never, "He showed me that he had a real good stop in him, and he went on to take the futurity with it." This type of trainer seems to have forgotten that without the horse, he's nothing.

Unsuccessful trainers tend to move around frequently. Six months seems to be about as long as they spend in one spot. The horses being handled by the unsuccessful trainer don't appear in the showring much. He always says, "They aren't much right now, but give me another month...."

Many people do want to use patience and work through problems, but ultimately lose their temper and throw gasoline on the fire. The horses that those people train never seem to improve. They stay on the same plateau of accomplishment.

Share credit and enjoy the ride when your horse does things right. Examine what you are doing when he does things wrong.

BUILD THOSE HORSEMANSHIP SKILLS

Although this book is about RESISTANCE FREE horse training, once you begin work under saddle, horsemanship skills are a big part of the equation. I feel you can't emphasize good hands and legs enough. You simply can't train a horse effectively without them. The horse responds to consistency and firmness, both of which come from good horsemanship. An unschooled trainer will never be as consistent a rider as will the person who learns a classical set of cues and can use them effectively. Horses trained by unschooled horsemen may operate from a set of cues that are unknown to others. Horses like this are hard to sell because no one else can ride them. Nobody else knows where the buttons are.

The Importance of Good Hands

The rider's hands have a lot to do with a horse's attitude under saddle. They create trust and security, like the rudder on a ship. Hands are a physically small part of the rider, but are largely responsible for the guidance of the whole works.

An important factor in good horsemanship is the ability to know when to give slack and when to take it up, so as not to override the horse. A horse can never become light if he is ridden with heavy aids throughout his training. Instead he will be waiting for that thump on the ribs, that heavy pull on the rein.

The RESISTANCE FREE trainer develops a command of feel through the fingertips, not the fists. Riding is a process of constantly adjusting rein length and contact, obtaining yields, and making further adjustments. Meanwhile the hands themselves stay in a square that is about six to eight inches in size. Don't let your hands float all over the place, and don't let them get too fast. Always work your hands in coordination with your legs.

Soft, slow hands give the horse a tremendous amount of confidence and a very trusting attitude. A rider with hurried hands that snatch in abrupt signals will make nervous horses that fall into the rider's hands at the slightest provocation. Your hands account for about 40 percent of your riding ability. Hands create attitude, and, ultimately, confidence. The forearm extends through the wrist and fingers to give you direct feel of the horse's mouth. The hand is a continuation of the arm. Through the reins, the hand operates directly on the bit, and the severity of the bit depends on the finesse of the user. (Always start a young horse in a mild bit. We'll look into bitting issues later in Chapter Five.)

The fingers hold the reins in a relaxed, firm manner, with the same amount of tension as you would use when holding a pencil. Naturally the position differs! The fingers offer finesse in riding, and the hands are responsible for more obvious motions. Good riders are constantly making adjustments to the reins and the horse's position. They never ride along with a frozen grip. However, these movements are discreet and nearly invisible, except to the experienced eye.

Use the hands in harmony with the rest of the body to give the horse confidence and prepare him for each movement. For this to work, you must have slow, quiet hands with straight wrists. When the wrist is bent, the tendons lose their flexibility and ability to follow the horse. Do your horse a favor and focus on developing effective hands.

When the rider rides on a solid foundation of seat and legs coupled with good hands, every horse he rides is actually being trained every ride. When done well, good horsemanship creates a feeling of unity. If ridden badly, the horse's training can desert him and he will go downhill in a hurry. Develop your skills so you can create harmony, not chaos, in your horse.

The Rider's Legs

The rider's legs and feet really give the horse solid trust and confidence in the rider. It's like taking a child's hand as you walk across the street. The child receives friendship and security through your hand. Your horse can get similar reassurance if your legs and feet provide reliable contact and communication. The rider who has good leg rhythm and is able to follow the horse's beat at all gaits will develop horses that are consistent in their **cadence** and **rhythm**. As we discussed earlier about hands, you can't create it if you can't ride it. Disorganized legs lead to disorganized horses.

A helpful demonstration in the importance of rhythm is to stand and shake hands with someone. Both of you should pick up a matching rhythm. Notice how easy and comfortable the hand shaking process is. Next, one of you should start to shake hands twice as fast while the other one maintains the original rhythm. This demonstrates how very easily unity is disrupted when two partners are out of sync. Good horsemanship really depends on finding and maintaining reliable rhythm with your horse.

You can begin to tune into the rhythms of the horse's footfalls in your groundwork. The RESISTANCE FREE rider can pick up the rhythm of footfalls when doing the Clock Drill on the ground (we'll cover that in Chapter Four) to move the horse's hips (hindquarters). Observe how the legs cross over and engage. When you work in the training pen, match your walk to the horse's steps while you drive the horse. Later, when you work in the saddle, maintaining rhythm becomes automatic because of your practice with rhythm on the ground. If you can't get it on the ground, you won't get it on the horse, so really work on this.

The leg should gather the horse just as a whisk broom gathers dirt. Use the leg in a light press, press, and press motion, rather than one long, deadening squeeze that the horse can easily tune out. Each press of the calf should be in rhythm with the horse's steps. The rider's leg is used correctly when the bulging calf muscle provides steadiness and confidence. Leg cues don't come from the knee or the heel. The lower leg works like a drumbeat. It should be positioned beneath the rider, the optimum place for its controlled use. Riders who are insecure in their legs and feet produce horses that are frustrated and lack cadence. Develop this ability as a rider so that you can give the young horse the best start under saddle.

As a rider, you also need awareness of which side of your body is the strongest. Many riders are strong on the left side and are puzzled by their horse's distinct preference for the right lead. Recognize your own imbalances and how they affect the horse. Don't blame him for responding to the cues you send unaware of what you are doing. Many do not realize just how sensitive the horse is to the rider's body language. If he can feel a fly on his hip, he can feel you tighten up or lean, whether deliberately or not.

continued on page 28

SPURS

I always ride with spurs. That doesn't mean they're always in use...but they're there. Before you add them to your boots, make sure you've got your legs under complete control so every use of this training tool is deliberate and only as strong as necessary. Spurs provide an enforcement of "forward" when necessary. As long as the horse is responding to the press-release of the calf muscle, you won't need to use them, but spurs serve as an excellent back-up if the horse tunes you out. When you use the spur too much, though, the red-light response is tail wringing. Back off. Spurs are an aid, not an end in themselves (figs. 2.1 to 2.5).

After using the spur as a reinforcement, repeat the transition or exercise, this time without the aid of the spur, to give the horse the opportunity to respond to the calf alone and demonstrate that he understands the progressive nature of aids. If he ignores your leg, apply the spur. The horse is no fool and will eventually grasp the idea that if he moves to the nudge of the calf, he will avoid the spur contact. This is the kind of learning you want to look for and encourage in your horse. (We'll explore other under-saddle lessons in Chapters Six and Seven.)

2.1 This Western spur with the shorter shank and dull rowel is for a young, or sensitive horse.

2.2 This longer-shanked Western spur should only be used by an experienced rider on a fully trained, lazy horse.

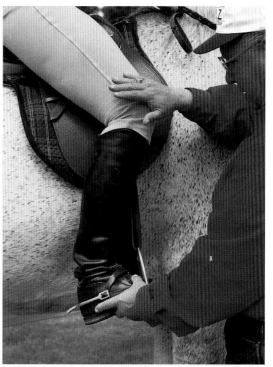

2.3 (Top left) The English spur for the sensitive, or young horse.

2.4 (Top right) The English spur for the lazy, or heavy-sided horse placed in a normal calf position.

2.5 (Bottom right) On some lazy horses you may need to place the spur further back on the horse's barrel a few times for effect, before resuming your normal calf position.

The rider should not stand in the stirrups or bounce from side to side, but sit solidly, stable on the horse. He will create steady performance by using his feet and back to push the horse in a forward motion. This skill does not arrive without good horsemanship basics. The horse knows exactly where the rider's body weight will be from moment to moment when the rider develops an independent seat. This rider will be able to progress much more quickly with his horses than the horseman who is as unstable as a sack of potatoes ever can.

Before you begin to introduce a young horse to actual work under saddle, make sure your riding skills are up to the task of giving your horse the support and balance he will need from you. My book RESISTANCE FREE *Riding* (see Resources) offers much more information than I have room for here. If you're still building your skills, there is no shame in finding a talented friend or professional to bolster your horse's confidence in the beginning. Get him started right—that is, RESISTANCE FREE—and your horse will soon be able to take care of you while you polish your abilities along with his.

Don't ever judge the rider who tries but fails. Judge only those who fail to try.

START WITH THE RIGHT HORSE

In many instances, horse selection determines your ultimate success or failure as a trainer. You can save yourself a lot of time and stress by choosing wisely instead of emotionally. Before you ever step out the door to go horse hunting, you must first decide what direction you want to go in with the horse. If you have dreams of competing at the top levels, you'll need a horse that can help get you there. And if you're looking to develop a savvy, sane trail partner, you probably won't want to choose a highly bred "General" horse. The next sections will cover the basics of matching a prospect to your plans for him wisely, based on his breeding, attitude, and conformation.

Write down the goals you have for the horse you select. If you're looking for a pleasure horse, a reiner, or a cutter, remember that today's competitive horse is so specialized that there are specific bloodlines with aptitudes for these events. Look at the bloodlines that are winning in that division, and go to those breeders to shop. That's a good start. Don't shortcut your homework if you intend to be successful at the top levels with the horse you train. Do plenty of research before you put your money down. If you intend to compete in the breed shows, is this the breed you want to be involved with? If your goal is the open competitions where breed is not a factor, then you need only focus on the qualifications of the individual horse.

One of the typical novice mistakes is to buy "color." Most novices read all of the Black Stallion books and saw the movies, and of course, what do they want? Or, they want a horse like Trigger. Experienced people make different mistakes in selecting horses. Maybe they want a pleasure champion, but they select a horse that moves like a Holstein cow. Or they are looking for a reining horse and the one they pick is so high behind that it can hardly keep a saddle on. To be successful on a consistent basis, first choose a horse that is built to do the job.

If it's a factor in your plans, consider which breed you wish to work with. Granted, most breeds are capable of doing nearly anything in an adequate fashion, but it's unlikely that you would select a Clydesdale if you are interested in the National Reining Horse Finals. If you want to train an open jumper, a Tennessee Walker is not as likely a prospect as a Thoroughbred or a warmblood. Outstanding individuals have been successful in disciplines not usually performed by their breed, but to stack the deck in your favor explore breeds with histories of success if you want to climb the levels in your chosen sport.

Next you must select the right horse within the breed for the activity you have chosen. After all, if you wanted to be a stock-car racer, you wouldn't purchase a Volkswagen. It also follows that you wouldn't buy an Indy car for shuttling your kids from school to practice. Yet people make that sort of mistake all the time when buying horses. They assume that any horse can do anything and operate on that premise. If it has four legs, it will do!

Most breeds, however, have some diversity in type that is specifically tailored to particular events. For example, Morgans come in two general types. There are the traditional Morgans, with bulkier body structure, and the Saddlebred-type Morgans, with a finer conformation geared to a showier performance. Both types compete side by side in many classes, but in certain divisions, one type will have the edge over the other. There's similar variation with the Arabian breed. The horses that make Park champions are quite unlike the ones who do Hunter Hack or Trail. Their attitudes and their movement are different. If you've got a dream one way or another, choose your prospect accordingly. Here are some selection tips that have worked for me over the years.

Rating Young Stock: Attitude

So how do you narrow the candidates once you've decided which direction you want to head in? Let's assume that you're shopping for a weanling at this point, so that you can do all of the training work correctly and not have to patch up somebody else's mistakes. A good beginning is to look at young horses moving freely in a group. Of course this is just about the only option you have with weanlings and yearlings, as they are not yet broke. But even with older stock, you can get a good idea of what you are looking at this way.

Encourage them to mill around. Don't put them into a frenzy and get them hurt, just stir them up a bit. After a few minutes they will sort themselves out. You'll notice there is a dominant horse, the General, and there is a bunch who kind of play "follow the leader," and there will be the lowly Private at the bottom of the **pecking order,** covered with "obedience medals"—bite marks—all over his body.

Have in mind what you are looking for at all times. If you are looking for a speed-event horse, or a reiner, or something in a sport that demands a lot of initiative and courage, you shouldn't be afraid to pick the youngster who is out in front of the pack.

If you choose to do Pleasure or Trail with the "General" horse, though, that could be a nightmare. A dominant horse that doesn't want to be passed by anybody—think about it. Even if he works well, his "I'm the Boss" attitude will constantly reflect displeasure with the proximity of the other horses, whatever they are doing. On the other hand, he might make a terrific racehorse.

It's a tradition that the General makes a good futurity horse because he is aggressive, smart, and has the extra sting to win the big one. Unfortunately he'll also take about four times as long to train. If you have a barn full of Generals, you can only ride about a quarter as many horses as you would otherwise. I have found over the years that you need to be very assertive in your groundwork before you ever get on. This type of self-assured horse is going to require a lot more body language and communication on your part to accept that you're in charge.

I had always been told to look for the leader—the General, the one who's top of the herd. I remember that all the books I read when I was younger said that you would have a superstar when that willful horse finally came around. Well, twenty-five years later, I had a different view. Who wants to spend that kind of time? I decided to go clear to the other end of the pecking order, and I looked for the horse who was already taking orders from everybody else. Surely this would be my superstar.

I learned that this wasn't the answer, either. This horse lacked character and self-confidence, and no amount of work was going to instill them. His training didn't stick, either. What he learned on Monday was forgotten by Wednesday. Or if it did stick, he would not be able to take pressure. At a big futurity, he might make the cut into the finals, but he wouldn't be able to stand the pressure and would cave in like a house of cards. He might be nervous and insecure, or he could get sullen. He clearly wasn't designed to be top horse if pressure was involved. However, the meek horse that is always at the bottom would be a good prospect for a trail riding horse. He wouldn't race the other horses all the time, nor would he get out of control if another horse came up behind him. He wouldn't have any competitiveness to get in the way of your needs.

So now that I'm older and wiser, I look for intelligence, balance, and a horse that is in the middle of the ranks. The Captain, say, as opposed to the General. When you go out to the corral, this horse is the first one to raise his head. He will probably have one or two horses between him and you because he's not totally sure of your intentions. Pick up a small stone and throw it. He'll be the first one to take notice and watch it.

Next, separate the colt you like from the others and see how he behaves. Is he secure enough to stand and watch you, or is he in a panic to get back to the safety and comfort of the herd? I have a tendency to go with the horse that can be independent—he doesn't crash the fence to try and get back to the others. This behavior tells you whether he's got a "ten" in self-confidence or a "three." The horse that panics in an attempt to go back to the others should be reconsidered, if courage and independence are on your list of preferred characteristics.

Another of my tests is to crowd the herd into a corner. If the horse I'm interested in stands back into the corner, raises his head, and watches me, I'll pay a lot more money for him. If, on the other hand, this horse breaks away when I

put pressure on the group and runs between me and the fence when there are only a couple inches of daylight between us, he could definitely be a liability under pressure. I personally don't want to put a lot of time into him. After all, his choice was to leave when the going got tough. So I let him go, and pick another one.

I observe how a youngster handles himself and how he interacts and socializes, because these herd behaviors are important clues as to how he will be to train. I recommend that if your personality is strong or demanding, look for the horse that is a little less demanding—a laid-back horse. If your personality is quiet, you're more likely to get along better with the horse who has more quickness and sensitivity.

Balance is Key

Back in the pen, always watch those "babies" as they move. I could write an entire book on movement, but the key is balance. Look for the one who changes leads cleanly front and behind, and lopes little circles in good balance. He should have good cadence, use his back well, and have his hocks underneath him.

It doesn't hurt to have a piece of paper and a pencil to use in scoring babies on a 1 to 10 basis. My 9 and 10 babies will be of real quality; the 5, 6, and 7 colts are okay. Anything lower than a 5 isn't usually a prospect.

When I walk into the pen, maybe I see a colt do a little circle, change leads, maybe do a rollback and keep his balance. That's probably a 9 or a 10 right there. If I see him bouncing off fences, dropping hind leads or not changing at all, he'll score anywhere from 4 to 6, depending on his overall quality.

Carefully observe the youngster's conformation. Avoid crooked-legged horses. The horse that has one or both forelegs cocked outward, as if to turn one direction or the other, is subject to stress in his knee joints and other potentially major problems.

Every great horseman will tell you that correctness is like a pillar holding up a roof. The more correct he is the sounder he will be. No matter what sport you are interested in, every prospect needs to have athletic ability and a balanced structure.

THE PERFECT "10"

In my career as a judge and clinician, I have had the opportunity to see some of the most athletic horses in the world. I've been curious about the ingredients of greatness and always very interested in how the owners of great horses have been able to develop the eye to select these super horses.

There's a lot of pressure when a client provides you with a blank check and asks you to find them the best horse out there. I found out that developing a good eye could make the difference between a long or very short career. Being at the right place at the right time helped a lot. So did having access to lots of great horses to evaluate and measure. Eventually I came up with a system of my own that gave me some very reliable indications of a prospect's potential for success. Here's how I evaluate prospects against the scale of the perfect 10.

Attitude

I was judging the American Quarter Horse Association (AQHA) World Show with Tom Finley, breeder of Doc Bar, the legendary Quarter Horse who became a great sire of cutting horses that were brilliant, intense, and intelligent. Tom told me one afternoon in the judge's room that when Doc Bar was just a foal, he would watch everything that moved. Tom felt that curiosity was a sign of intelligence: the more curious the horse, the smarter he was. I factored that idea into the tests I now use to evaluate the attitude and trainability of any horse at any age.

1. First, attitude: I pick up a clump of dirt and stand at the prospect's side. I drop the dirt out to the side and I look for his response. If he immediately looks and is curious, I give him a score of 10. If he looks and then loses interest, he gets a 5. If he doesn't notice anything, this horse gets a zero (fig. 2.6).

2. Next, tolerance: I firmly push on the bridge of the nose. If he gives at the poll with a level head, he gets a 10. If he pushes against my hand and then gives, his score is 5. If he resists and doesn't give at all, zero (fig. 2.7).

3. Then I pull softly on the halter to the left. If he gives easily to quiet pressure and keeps his head level, his score is 10. If he raises his head while giving, I give him a 5. No give earns him 0 points. Then I repeat this test with about three pounds of pressure and score his responses the same way (figs. 2.8 and 2.9).

4. Lastly, I rub my thumb in firm circles ten times on each side of his barrel, starting at his elbow and going along his belly. Each time he resists or pops his tail, I deduct one point (fig. 2.10).

These simple tests give me a good idea of how trainable he'll be. A horse without a trainable attitude is like a car with a dead battery.

Measurements to Predict Athletic Ability

This system measures and predicts physical potential in performance horses of all ages. Cutters, reiners, and other horses that need to be extremely athletic should earn very high scores. The performance requirements for pleasure and recreational horses aren't as rigorous, so scores can be a bit lower for them. These scores indicate where a horse's natural talents are, as allowed by his conformation. If

2.6 to 2.10 Attitude Tests

2.6 Attitude Test 1: Drop some dirt to the side to check your horse's curiosity level. This filly is showing interest.

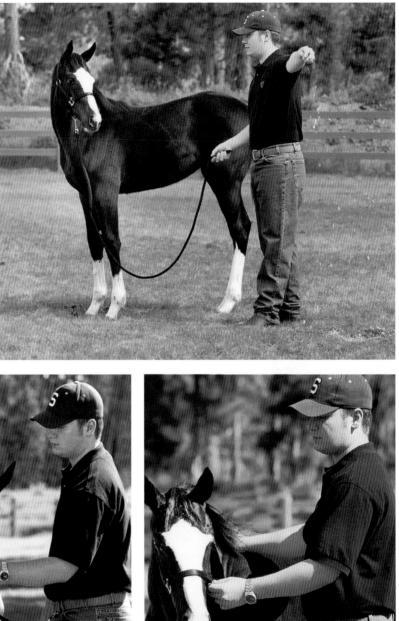

2.7 Attitude Test 2: Push directly on the nose and look for a soft bend in the poll.

2.8 Attitude Test 3: Pull the halter softly, looking for a level, even turn. If his head lifts, that's a "red light."

2.9 Attitude Test 4: Repeat Test 3 and increase your pressure on the halter to the equivalent of a weight of about three pounds.

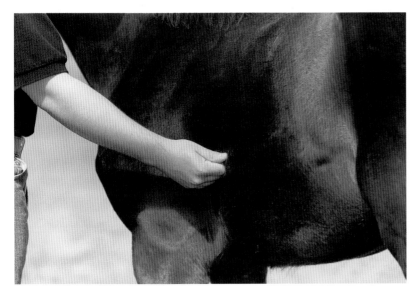

2.10 Attitude Test 5: Rub your thumb in firm circles from the girth along to the belly, ten times on each side.

you select a horse based on his potential and abilities for the job you have in mind, you're well on your way to success the RESISTANCE FREE way, because Nature will have given that horse the basics he needs to meet your requests.

Be aware that for Test 4 (comparing the foreleg length from the elbow to the ground, to the length of the hind leg from the stifle to the ground), this measurement is most reliable when applied to mature horses, generally over three years of age. The relationship between foreleg and hind leg lengths may fluctuate in the formative years, because they often grow at different rates until a horse achieves full height.

Set the horse up so he stands squarely on level ground. Use a piece of baling twine or a short rope to make the following comparative measurements for a balance assessment.

1. Measure the circumference of the throatlatch (fig. 2.11). Then measure the center of the chest to the middle of the withers (fig. 2.12). For a perfect 10, the throatlatch circumference should be half of the length of this measurement. If these lengths are the same, the score is zero.

   A clean, small throatlatch in the right proportion to the neck measurement allows the horse to easily break over at the poll as he gives to the bridle.

2. Compare the length of the underside of the neck to the topline neck measurement (figs. 2.13 and 2.14). If the bottom measures half of the top of the neck, give him a 10. If the measurements are equal, the score is zero.

   A long topline from poll to withers allows easier use of the shoulders—important for hunters, reiners, and **dressage** horses. A good score here is a must for excelling in these sports.

3. Measure from the middle of the loin to the middle of the withers to get the back measurement (fig. 2.15). This back-meas-

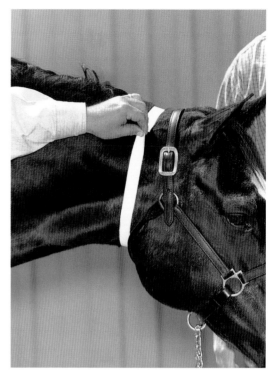

2.11 to 2.19 Balance Assessment Tests

2.11 Balance Assessment Test 1: Set the horse up squarely on level ground. Measure the complete circumference of the throatlatch. For a perfect 10 this measurement should be half the measurement shown in Test 2 (fig. 2.12).

urement length should be two-thirds of the neck measurement as seen in fig. 2.14 for a perfect 10 as you can see in fig. 2.16. If it's more than two-thirds, score in a *descending* scale from 10 down to zero—a zero being awarded for a back measurement that is the same, or longer, than the neck measurement.

A good score here is also a must for reiners and dressage horses.

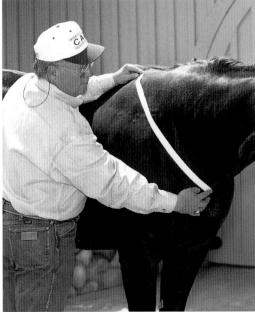

2.12 Test 2: Measure from the middle of the withers to the center of the chest. For every inch this measurement is more than half the throatlatch measurement in Test 1 (fig. 2.11), deduct one point. This ratio indicates how easy it will be for the horse to break at the poll and give to the bridle.

2.13 Test 3: Measure from the throatlatch to the center of the chest.

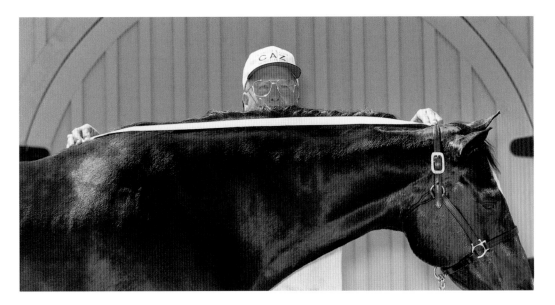

2.14 Test 4: The neck measurement from the top of the poll to the middle of the withers should ideally be twice the distance measured in Test 3 (fig. 2.13).

2.15 Test 5: Measure from the middle of the withers to the middle of the loin to get the back measurement.

2.16 Test 6: The back measurement in Test 5 (fig. 2.15) should equal two-thirds of the length of the neck measurement starting from the middle of the withers. This mare is a perfect 10.

2.17 Test 7: Measure from the top of the elbow down to the ground.

2.18 Test 8: Measure from the middle of the stifle to the ground. This should equal the measurement of the elbow to the ground in Test 7 (fig. 2.17) for a perfect 10.

4. Next, compare the length from the elbow to the ground with the measurement of the stifle to the ground (figs. 2.17 and 2.18). For a 10, these measurements should be identical. If he's higher behind, his score could be between 5 and zero, depending on how much higher. However, if he's higher in front, he gets more than a 10.

Horses that are lower in front will need to raise their heads for balance, which automatically hollows the back. A high score in this area is very important for Western-pleasure horses, hunters under-saddle, reining, barrel-racing, and roping horses. Strong dressage prospects also do best with a good score here. When the horse measures the same front and back, it will be easier for him to engage from behind to provide the impulsion so important in reining and dressage. If he is an inch or two higher in front, he really has potential to excel in these de-manding sports.

5. Equine geometry: Next, evaluate his shoulder and hindquarter angles by "building" a trapezoid, as demonstrated (fig. 2.19). Again, be sure he's set up squarely on level ground.

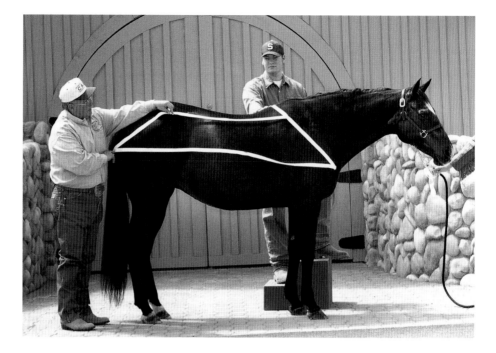

2.19 Test 9: The trapezoid should show the same shoulder and hip angles, and the bottom side should be twice as long as the top side. This measurement is good predictor of the horse's stride length.

You can use the trapezoid measurements to help identify the potential performance strengths of a foal as young as three-weeks old. When the base of the trapezoid is more than twice as long as the topline, this horse will have a long stride. His conformation may be best suited to cross-country, hunter, dressage, or racing sports. Basically, this horse might do his best work as an English prospect, where long strides will help him excel.

When the bottom of the trapezoid is *less* than twice the length of the top, the resulting shorter stride may make the horse better suited to Western sports, perhaps as a roper, or reiner. In those sports, his short, quick strides will be a real asset.

Adding It Up

There are a couple of ways you can use the scores that you've collected to determine whether a particular horse has what it takes to help you reach your goals. First, to get a picture of the prospect's overall potential, add the scores together and divide the total by the number of categories you've evaluated, which results in the combined average of the scores. For instance, if you collected nine scores that add up to 74 points, divide 74 by 9. The average is 8.2. That's a respectable score. Scores of 8 and above indicate the prospect will be both athletic and very trainable. If the score is between 5 and 7, you may have to work a bit harder to improve that horse's potential. Generally, I don't recommend buying a prospect with an average score below 5.

You can also evaluate individual scores to assess his potential for a specific discipline. For instance, if you want to develop a reining horse and the prospect has a good score in both the topline and length-of-back measurements, these strong scores might offset a poor mark in a less important area that would lower his average score. Assessing specific results can give you an idea of which skills may be natural to the horse and which areas you may have to really focus on improving with your training.

Let these results help you select the ideal horse among several prospects. Use the scores to develop a training plan that takes his strengths and weaknesses into account, and keep your expectations realistic. Don't assume that a horse that happens to be two inches higher behind will be able to effortlessly shift his weight back as he works a cow, for instance. Instead, while you train, use your new understanding of his assets and liabilities to develop the skills he'll need to succeed as a performance horse.

Now that you know more about his trainability and performance potential, inspect the horse's veterinary records, and don't hesitate to have a vet look over your prospect. Let the vet know your plans, so he can offer a professional opinion as to whether this horse's structure is appropriate for the activity. Veterinarians who work on performance horses have clear ideas about what goes wrong most often on horses in each type of work and can sometimes warn you that a horse's hocks won't stand up to sliding stops, or a right front tendon looks a little "iffy" so speed events are out. In some situations, X rays may be advisable to help detect hidden problems. Naturally, some of these particular factors diminish in importance when it comes to the horse you already own.

One of the things you can do that will make you a better evaluator of horses, including your own, is to spend a day with your farrier and your veterinarian. Seeing other horses and getting a professional assessment of them will give you a wider perspective that allows you to logically rate your own horses and prospects you are considering. There is no better way to educate yourself. Most farriers and vets are willing to have you along if you hold a few horses for them.

Another educational field trip is a visit to a local horse auction. Over the course of several auction visits you can be virtually guaranteed to see every unsoundness and blemish in the book, in every possible combination.

Evaluating the Horse You Have

In evaluating the horse you already have, perform the same assessment as if he were the horse you are considering buying. You have to be able to "read" him and evaluate his movement and conformation in order to avoid building unrealistic expectations for him. Assessment is a bit easier with the horse you have, because you eliminate the decision-making process. You've already selected the breeding. You own him. By the same token, you don't have a vet evaluation to worry about, unless you choose to have him rated for potential problems by the vet.

Resale value will be created by what you do with the horse. The better trained your horse is, the more value he will have. A horse that has been started with RESISTANCE FREE training will be very salable because anyone will be able to ride him. Many other training techniques aren't as universal when it comes to putting a new rider in the saddle.

"Barn blindness" is a common affliction among horse owners. Very few of us can objectively evaluate our own horses. Even if you "know" the faults and problems with your own horse, you begin to overlook them as time passes because they're so familiar. The person who works with only one horse typically doesn't get the multiple exposures to horses that develop a more balanced view of conformation. If your own horse has a host of blemishes and bumps, you may not even notice them after a while. They're just always there. On the other hand, a person who has never worked the horse before will immediately notice a blemish because it will stand out like a sore thumb.

You have to be realistic and honest with yourself. If your horse has a lot of problems or potential problems, you are faced with the decision of whether he will be a workable prospect or whether it's time to cut your losses and look for another horse better suited to your goals.

With the horse you already own, you clearly won't have a choice as to age. Depending on his maturity, you'll have to evaluate whether your horse is mentally ready to take on the demands of training, which I'll talk more about in general in Chapter Three. Readiness varies with each horse, just as the ability to learn differs in people.

Set up a balance sheet for your horse, putting pluses on one side and minuses on the other. Yes, he's that beautiful shade of gun-metal gray you've always wanted, and he has the best mane and tail you've ever seen...but his croup is higher than his withers, one hock is capped, and the windpuffs grow like mushrooms when you exercise him.

If you don't list at least three times as many assets as detriments, this horse should probably be reconsidered for the purposes you have in mind. You are going to have a hard time maintaining a positive mental attitude and excitement about the training process if you are dealing with a horse who isn't going to keep up with your demands. After all, if the horse can't learn or improve, it leads to frustration on your part, and a frustrated trainer is not going to get the most out of the horse. You also need to consider whether it's fair to ask the horse to try and achieve goals he's just not suited for. In my opinion, this is abuse of the worst sort. If he isn't constructed to allow him to collect and use his hindquarters, it's plain wrong to try to force him beyond the liabilities of his conformation. So be honest with your evaluation. If you have your heart set on keeping this horse, then you may need to adjust your goals for him in light of your assessment of his potential.

Don't be afraid to get a second opinion on your horse. Have other experienced horse people drop by and tell you their honest thoughts about him. And don't be afraid to put a value on your own time when you're calculating your balance sheet. A horse who trains twice as fast as another will give you a greater return on your time and effort than the horse who only learns one thing at a time...and forgets three others. It doesn't cost you any more to feed a good horse than a bad horse, so why not make sure you have the best horse you can afford? However, horses who are assessed as having many bad qualities and few good ones can be greatly changed throughout the course of their training when the trainer emphasizes only the good traits in their work. Over time, more and more good traits will appear.

If you have a personality clash with your horse, seriously consider looking further for your superstar. Most people can't get along with absolutely everybody they meet, and the same is true of horses. On the other hand, sometimes the right horse gets together with the right person and they can really rise to the top of the competition. Try and figure out honestly whether or not you're that person for your horse.

Don't let sentiment interfere with your plans. Just because Uncle Charley gave him to you, or because you love him a lot, or because he's part of the family, don't let that interfere with a realistic decision as to this horse's future in your barn. If you can evaluate him objectively and live with his liabilities while you enhance his strengths with RESISTANCE FREE training, then keep him and develop him into the best horse he can be.

So to sum up, when you evaluate your horse:

1. Don't be "barn blind."

2. Get a second opinion.

3. Make a balance sheet of pros and cons.

4. Evaluate whether the horse is able to meet your long-term goal in your chosen event.

5. Assess if he is able physically and mentally to learn the movements you require easily and well, no matter who is riding him.

2.20 Adjust your technique to match the horse you're working with—stallion, mare, or gelding. Note my square shoulders, raised hand, and erect body are getting this stallion's attention.

> *Don't assume blame for the temperament your horse was born with. He may simply be a difficult horse. Your task is to rise to the challenge, RESISTANCE FREE.*

STALLIONS, GELDINGS, AND MARES ALL TRAIN DIFFERENTLY

It's a common misconception that all horses train alike, whatever their sex. That's not the case. You have to adjust your technique to match the horse you are working with, as well as tailor it to any individual quirks he or she may have. For example, in the photo (fig. 2.20), my square shoulders, raised hand, and erect

body get this stallion's attention and keep his focus on me. With a mare, my body language could be softer without losing her focus. Sadly enough, over the years we've never really recognized this difference. It hasn't been written, or talked about much. We've just noticed that some trainers do really well with mares, others are fantastic with stallions, and some only work with geldings. A lot of this has to do with personality types, as well as how individual trainers adjust the use of their body language to fit various training scenarios.

We've all seen the trainer who has one method for doing everything and it doesn't change, no matter what he's got in the barn. Someone with narrow tactics like this will produce only mediocre results. I find that the trainer who is sensitive to the differences, particularly when working with a mare, is the trainer who will become very, very successful.

Stallions

The person who is very dominant, a quick mover, extremely powerful in personality—a type A—is without question the kind of person that gets along best with stallions. Many times that assertive type-A personality relates well with a stallion because, number one, in order for a stallion to be trained, he has to be submissive to you. This means that you have to establish yourself without doubt at the head of the pecking order.

Most stallions will challenge you twenty-four hours a day, seven days a week. This is just the way they're made up. I often tell people it's like someone standing on the edge of a bridge or a high building, looking down, weak-kneed. Can that individual control that feeling? Of course he can't. It's the same way with a stallion. He can't control that attitude that goes through him, saying "Be dominant, take control, be in charge." That's always going to be there. A successful stallion handler will be able to read his body language, noting the lift of the head or push of the shoulder that is a precursor to a more serious challenge. Some stallions will go as far as to strike, or swing their haunches at you, when you enter their stall. You have to be right on top of things. The person who is active and quietly aggressive, taking the offensive by moving the horse's shoulders and hips as I explained on page 15, makes sure that the stallion fails in his attempts to take charge.

When riding a stallion, you can sometimes feel him seem to gain weight under you. This feeling can be interpreted as him getting mad, but mostly it is a red light that warns you to start getting that horse back under control.

A real timid person who is forgiving and sits back and waits a lot won't be successful at training a stallion. If you let the stallion control your space or take advantage of you, in the blink of an eye he'll be running things. The timid person won't get a lot out of the stallion because he isn't in charge. The personality that prefers to watch instead of do will get in trouble because he becomes a following trainer instead of a leadership trainer. When a stallion is involved, that's a volatile combination. So if you need to work with a stallion, be prepared to do what it takes to be at the top of the pecking order—or else let someone else work with that horse.

When you work with a stallion, the training process goes faster, with less frustration and tension, if you work him in a quiet environment. Try to make sure there's minimum of horse traffic—or, better, none at all—to distract him from your work. He's got a short attention span that distractions make even shorter. So help him keep his mind on you by setting him up to focus clearly on your work so he's able and willing to follow your lead.

Geldings

Perhaps 80 percent of the horses shown and used today are geldings. They are particularly popular on ranches, as driving horses, and schoolhorses. Geldings tend to be very reliable. Some ranchers won't even let you bring a mare on to the place for a trail ride, but a spayed mare would fall into the same category of reliability as geldings, but there are far fewer of them.

A gelding trainer doesn't have to be quite as sharp as if he were working with a stallion or assertive mare. The pecking order will always be an important factor with horses, but most geldings can handle a wider range of challenges because of their steadiness, dedication, and persistence. A gelding somewhere in the middle of the dominance spectrum will be easiest to work with. He'll forgive mistakes and the trainer doesn't have to be wary or always on the alert, as with stallions. It's like when you drive down the middle of the road—you don't have to worry about sliding off the edges.

When training a gelding, repetition is a useful tool. He can take a little more drilling. Mares and stallions won't stand up to a lot of repetition. They lose patience and get mad more easily. Geldings don't show nearly as much temper. They also tend to be less distracted by the presence of other horses in neighboring paddocks and pens. They are not as protective of their space as are stallions and mares. When mounted, you can usually put a lot of pressure on a gelding before you run into red lights. A stallion is like a vapor of mist, always drifting in and out. Sometimes he's with you and sometimes he's not. The mare is easier to read.

If you put a gelding away after a problem day, things will probably work out okay the next day. Mares and stallions tend to remember things, particularly mistakes. When you quit, things had better be in order, or you will be facing trouble later, especially with a stallion.

Mares

I always consider myself an expert on the female of the species because I've raised two daughters! Females of any species require a slightly different approach.

With mares, when you run into resistance, you must back off and let them have their space. Unlike with a stallion, you have to wait and listen rather than dominate. If you challenge them and intrude on their space when you really should be backing off, you can go all the way to the other end of the spectrum and get nothing for your effort. Make sure you don't put pressure on a mare when you meet resistance. Back off, let her settle, and start again.

Be aware of the fact that some days even brushing them will irritate mares. Other days, very little bothers them. It changes from day to day and sometimes hour to hour, even during a training session. By waiting on a mare when

necessary, you'll notice that once you've established yourself as the dominant one in the relationship, she'll do anything in the world for you. Mares are a little more generous in going that extra mile. In this respect, they are superior to both the gelding and the stallion.

I find myself using the Pizza Theory often with mares. As I've said, this approach offers a little bit of new information at a time, in tiny bites that are easy for the horse to "swallow." You break down a problem or a new idea into the smallest possible increments and teach the horse each little step before moving on to the next one. So I tend to work with mares a little bit at a time, putting pressure in different places, finding out how much they can take that day, and gradually work up to 100 percent.

In training mares, you have to be cautious during your training and never set up a wreck. Make sure you read that mare well enough so that you back off before you get into a problem. It often means taking a deep breath and stepping away. Don't be quick around mares. They respond to slow movements. They are by nature both very giving and fragile; once bruised by a lost temper, they won't come back to your corner without a lot of nurturing over a long period of time.

The key to a mare is making sure she's on your side. You do that by taking a quiet, soft approach. If you use the same body language and quickness as with a stallion, you will be hitting locked doors. You might as well be working with an ice cube. Look for small steps of progress. If you read her right, there are no limits to her potential.

Mares don't allow many mistakes. A mistake will set a tone for the day that will devastate all your preceding work. You might bring a mare out, spend ten minutes getting her attitude right, do some work, have a problem, and spend another 45 minutes getting her back where to you were.

Mares are careful about other horses in the area. They are very, very sensitive to their surroundings. I like to make sure that the ring is quiet particularly with younger mares. They get triggered easily by a lot of commotion.

A mare that is cycling may be very hard to work with. If you ride a mare in heat, keep her alone. She won't work around other horses very well, particularly stallions. Some race trainers say that mares that are in heat generally do not race well during that time. It's the same way in showing. Let her have that time off. Of course there are exceptions to this. Some mares never tell you they're cycling and never miss a beat in training or competition. They're always right there, ready and waiting. Listen to your mare and respond accordingly.

A mare's disposition will change after she has had a foal. It will definitely change while she is carrying the foal. The new estrogen and hormone balances make a dramatic difference. I've seen many top show mares do well while in foal, have the foal, and after the foal is weaned and they return to training, become totally different horses. Their personalities change. Take the time to go back to the basics with your "new" mare to discover her limits, and she'll work with you in harmony once more.

Train with kindness.
The echoes will last for a lifetime.

CHAPTER 3

First Lessons

PLACES TO TRAIN

In the Stall

I learned some valuable lessons about ground-work from watching Thoroughbred trainers at the major breeding farms in Kentucky and Florida when I was in my late teens. It was quite a shock in the beginning to watch as weanlings and yearlings were worked without being hobbled or otherwise restrained. I began to realize then that there were other ways to do things than the ways I'd been brought up with.

Those babies were handled quietly. Much of their groundwork was done in a twelve by twelve foot stall with a dirt or mat floor, usually with shavings for bedding; straw bedding gets pretty slick and dangerous. These young Thoroughbreds were put under saddle and ridden for the first time in their stalls.

I've come to firmly believe that if you're going to train a horse, you need a stall. The stall provides a enclosed area that allows you to easily get your hands on him. Usually the horse can see out of the stall, making him more secure.

You can watch him, too. And, it can provide an important neutral zone for introducing him to his first lessons in groundwork and even under-saddle work, as I saw at the Thoroughbred farms. In Chapter Four, I'll suggest that most of his early lessons take place in the security of his stall.

When you start these lessons, keep distractions outside the stall to a minimum. Don't choose a stall in the breeding barn where the stallions are screaming. If there are mares in heat and stallions are present, the frustration level will be high all of the time. Keep your performance horses and horses in training together in a separate barn or aisle.

Training Pens

Having the right training area is important. If you're going to train, you need a round corral or a square pen. I like to use a pen at least 40 feet in diameter. In fact, the older I get, the more I like to start a horse in a pen that's about 45 feet, but for most work, 40 feet is a good minimum.

Many trainers use 60-foot round pens, giving the horse a lot of room to move. However, he's hard to turn and keep into a space. I think that a colt who is 90 to 120 days into training and doesn't have any problems, the 60-foot pen is great, but a 40- or 45-foot pen is better for starting.

It should have sand footing that packs just a little, unlike loose beach sand. I think a lot of us make the mistake of choosing footing in our training pens that is too soft. After just a few laps, the horse is exhausted. Remember that horses, especially young horses, are very subject to injuries such as pulled muscles and strained tendons, which occur easily in deep footing. Also, footing that is deep, soft, and uneven tends to work against you in training because the horse can't pick up a steady gait and hold it for any length of time. Deep footing does take the edge off of horses quickly and deters them from doing too much jumping around, but I don't believe that benefit offsets the potential for damage to tendons and ligaments. In general, about three inches of sand is enough. The horse keeps his gaits better and gets his balance more quickly. You definitely don't want hard, bare soil, with or without rocks, in your training pens. Repeated concussion on a hard surface also damages legs and hooves.

The training pen should be well drained. Otherwise, in wet weather conditions you won't get a lot of use out of it. Some farms put a cover over their round pens, like a gazebo. You should also have the ability to water the pen as necessary to keep the dust down.

I also prefer a pen horses can see out of, rather than a solid walled one. One of the things I learned early in my career on my father's ranch was that horses paid attention to you better in a solid walled pen. We had four pens to work in, some of which were twelve feet high. The drawback, however, was that when you took the horse out of the solid pen, it was like starting him all over again. He would spook at little things and you would have to reeducate him to pay attention to you. In addition, when he didn't have the wall or the rail to "steer" him, he could be very difficult to turn.

One year I was working some yearling futurity horses. My walled round pen flooded so I had to use some panels that I had around my hot walker to make a temporary pen. This enclosure was three rails high. The worst futurity horse I had that year came out of that pen he could see out of with a better attitude and rode better outdoors than my best horse produced in the solid walled pen. At that time I wrote an article about that and got a lot of feedback from the old cowboys, pointing out that the horse concentrated better in the solid pen. However, the progressive trainers commented that they had found the same thing. If a horse can see out of the pen, whether it is round or square, he will notice outside activities, such as other horses or animals moving around, and he will learn to deal with them. Mentally, he will be far more stable. Today's trainers use the open pens with great success.

I personally choose a square pen over a round pen. Often in a round pen, the horse uses the wall to balance off of, like a motorcycle doing a wall-of-death stunt. He leans on it, and when you take him outdoors, he has trouble getting his balance without the wall for assistance. The square pen encourages him to keep his shoulders up. The corners become an aid in teaching the horse to adjust his balance. When he learns to canter in the square pen, he learns to keep his body straight and level.

The training pen, square or round, should ideally be close behind the barn, or on one end. The less traffic in this area, the better. For the Four Phases of Training covered in this book, it's very important to keep distractions to a minimum. The pen should be smooth in construction so that you can turn a tacked-up horse loose inside and not worry about him catching his bridle on something. Gates should open outward rather than inward for safety and ease of operation. The latches should be easily operable from either side, and have no projections that might snag a horse's equipment.

The Training Arena

For an outside training arena, 120 by 200 feet is an ideal size. Again, I want a solid sand base with some bark dust to hold the moisture. In an arena that size you have an abundance of room for circling and a lot of rail for working the horse along. You can get by with a 60- by 120-foot ring if you're short of space. It's a good idea for the outside ring to be a little isolated from the training barn. You often raise some dust, and you don't need that dust going right into the barn and tack room. The extra grit and dirt will get into the horse's coats as well, and that's the last place you want it. Locate the arena downwind, a short ride away from the barn, if you can.

I personally prefer an arena rail about three-and-a-half feet high. Horses seem apprehensive about something coming down on them when the rail is over their head in a "bull-ring" effect. Because the rail is used a lot when schooling turnbacks, the horse does better if he has a little more room to position his head, which is possible with the lower rail. I like a rail that I can ride along and rollback into at any moment, low enough so that the horse can really use himself in a little cleaner way. He has a lot more freedom and doesn't bump his head all of the time. The corners in the arena keep his shoulders up.

The arena should have multiple gates so that you aren't limited to one gate for going in and out. Ideally, there should be gates at each end, and at least one on a side. This helps keep the horse from getting gate-sour. Each gate should be set up so that you can operate it from horseback. This teaches the horse to automatically get in position and that gate-opening is just part of life. He learns to sidepass, two-track, and to be patient. All of these lessons are important. A little extra money spent on gates provides you a super training tool.

You need to be able to get a tractor in to drag the arena, and if possible, the training pen, too. If you don't plan ahead for tractor access, you're going to find that holes, pits, and irregular footing are constant problems. For smaller enclosures, raking with a large landscape rake is a good substitute.

Ideally, you also need an irrigation system so that you can keep the footing sprinkled. Putting a sprinkler setup along the rails works very well. It's not good to work a horse in dry, dusty conditions all of the time. The dust will stress his respiratory system, causing him to snort and cough, which breaks focus as well as compromising his health. Dust doesn't do a thing for his coat, either. You should make this area as safe and as pleasant as possible so that he enjoys his work and stays healthy.

If you have an indoor arena, it should be in a separate building from where horses are stabled. Again, this keeps horses from being subjected to all that dust. A horse's stall should be a place of rest and privacy, and it's easier to provide that environment when it's in a separate structure from an indoor ring. Keep horse and people traffic to a minimum in the stall area.

EARLY TRAINING EQUIPMENT

It is extremely important to have the proper training equipment. You can't do the job right if you haven't got the tools you need. Let's begin by looking at basic tack for groundwork.

Since so much of the early work with your horse will be done while he's haltered, be sure that this important piece of tack fits him correctly. So many of us just put on a halter and don't pay attention to fit or adjustment. The fit is more important than whether the halter is made of nylon or leather, though leather has the advantage of breaking should your horse get caught somehow and fight against it. If you ignore how your halter (or any other tack, for that matter) fits, you throw away some of your tools for success before you ever start.

To be sure the halter fits, check that the cheek straps set right up next to the horse's cheekbones. The crown piece should rest in the poll groove behind the ears. A loose halter slides too far back on the horse's neck. When this happens you'll have just as much success as if you put a rope around his middle and try to lead him. The same applies to the noseband. A sloppy, loose noseband doesn't give clear signals. I like to see the halter fit snugly around the throatlatch, right next to the cheekbones. There should be no more than a half-inch gap, enough for a couple of fingers to slide alongside (fig. 3.1).

Each time a correctly fitted halter is pulled, a clean, crisp signal is sent to the horse's poll area. This preparatory command alerts the horse to the idea that we're about to make a request. There's a bonus result, too, because the massage action of the halter on the poll area releases endorphins, and, as I said in Chapter One, endorphins contribute a sense of comfort and well-being that automatically help keep the horse soft and the "lights green."

Next, you need a seven-foot, heavy, cotton lead rope, which is easy to grip. It's very useful in groundwork. Choose the heavy, cotton rope with enough weight to it so that you can start teaching the horse to work off of the slack right away. Remember, if he can feel a fly on his hip, he can feel you take the slack out of that rope. A thin lead rope doesn't give the same amount of signal.

Test this for yourself. Grasp a lightweight lead rope at one end and have someone else hold the other end. Close your eyes. Have the other person pick up the slack. Tell them when you can feel it. Then try it with a heavier lead. With the heavier rope, you'll feel the movement sooner.

I advise that you avoid choosing a lead rope with a bull snap and a lead chain. The snap is too heavy, giving the brakes-on effect, and it also bounces around at the trot, distracting the horse from what you are trying to teach him.

I use a 30-inch brass chain on horses beginning when they're yearlings. Pass the end of the chain through the near side cheek ring, under the chin, through the far cheek ring, and up to the side ring above the horse's eye to be fastened

3.1 A halter that fits correctly. The crown piece should rest in the poll groove behind the ears, and the noseband just below the cheekbone.

(figs. 3.2 and 3.3). This arrangement provides both poll pressure (command of the poll) and instant release of pressure. Without instant release, it's like driving a car with one foot on the brake all the time. Any mechanic will tell you that's a bad idea. Imagine what conflicting messages it sends to the horse.

Remember Richard's Rule Number 6 from Chapter One: "A good leader applies pressure within the boundaries of the horse's comfort zone for maximum learning." A good leader releases that pressure, too. As you train, keep in mind that the release of pressure is the reinforcement that tells the horse he made the right choice. No release, and he learns that the pressure remains, no matter what he does. This is the wrong message. Be sure that you use training tools to do a job. When the job is done, turn the tool off.

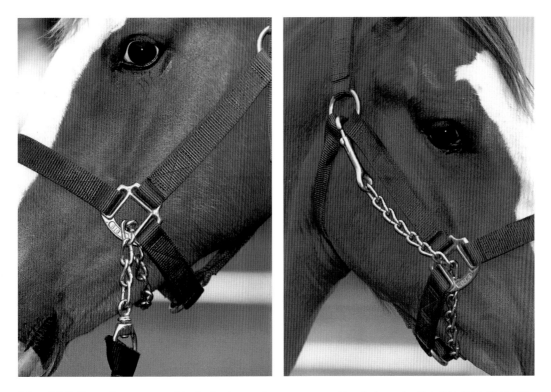

3.2 and 3.3 For poll pressure and instant release of pressure, pass the chain under the chin from the near side and attach it to the opposite upper jowl ring in this manner.

Putting the chain over the horse's nose is less effective. There are no significant nerve endings in that area, but there *are* branches of nerves under the chin that make the area far more sensitive. Some people who train say if you put the chain over a stallion's nose, that's for breeding, and under the chin is for working, and that the horse is supposed to know the difference. I have my doubts.

> *You will touch the future*
> *of every horse you train.*

MAKE SURE HE'S READY

Now it's time to assess your horse's readiness to begin the Four Phases of Training. Your horse will need to have mastered some basic skills before you begin his first RESISTANCE FREE lessons. Kindergarten prepares a child one step at a time for the routines of a classroom and provides both confidence and basic skills for successful learning down the road. Much the same way, the time you take with your horse's preschool education is important to ensure long-term success as a performance horse.

Is your horse "grown up" enough to take the physical side of training? The maturity of the body has a great deal to do with whether the horse will be able to accept the work. If he is hurting or feels that he can't take what's coming, he will have no interest in what you are doing—whether it be to him or with him.

And then there's his mental maturity to consider. These are the things I look for in determining whether a young horse is mentally ready to learn: does he stands quietly when tied? What is his response to other horses and people traffic? Does he seem really insecure? Is he able to focus throughout a 20-minute training session? If you've got **green lights** on all of those things, then he's ready to go to school, mentally.

If, on the other hand, he gets really nervous when other horses and people are around, won't stand quietly when tied, and tends to overreact to every little disturbance, he has some mental maturing to do before he's ready to accept more complicated work. A horse that only focuses for three or four minutes during a training session does not allow you to make significant progress. By the time you have his attention, he's almost ready to quit in his mind. These are **red lights** that tell you these things have to be fixed before you can go further.

However, even if he's not mature enough to start training as a saddle horse yet, you may find that the basic lessons in Chapter Four, when done in short sessions a little at a time, may help him learn to focus a little more each lesson. They'll also help you assess his physical maturity. As a bonus, you may find the immature young horse gains in self-confidence. Every time you use positive reinforcement to make **"Security Deposits,"** he'll become more interested in the process that earns him the praise and reassurance you provide.

Teach Patience Through Tying

Let's look at teaching a green horse to tie. Remember, horses are genetically programmed to flee danger. Understand that a horse that is tied has lost one of his most basic tools for survival, so especially in the first lessons, be patient and reward the smallest efforts toward cooperation. Avoid situations that might trigger his instinct to flee. Some young horses get the idea of hanging around without much trauma. Others need a lot of time, patience, and positive reinforcement. This is an extremely important lesson, so take the time to teach it well.

By the time a horse is a yearling, you should be able to tie him anywhere and have him just stand and wait. To begin, put leg protection on him. It's always better to be safe than sorry. If you've got an older horse whose a pro at standing around, tie him near the youngster to provide security and reinforcement. I like to tie up to a solid wall and to some kind of a rubber inner tube with give to it. This way, if he jumps forward or steps up, or whatever, he won't really hurt himself. If he does pull back and run into the wall, he is not likely to put his foot into something and get caught in it. I tie with a seven-foot long, thick, cotton rope, just a little above his head. Always use a quick-release knot. Don't "hang" him; tie him just high enough to keep him from getting his legs tangled in the rope, and keep him safe and quiet. Make sure that when you tie a horse, you use common sense. If the weather is hot, don't tie him in the sun. Your goal is to teach him patience, not suffering.

The first few times you tie him, stay nearby. Rub him on the shoulder. Release some calming endorphins by rubbing his jowls, above his eyes, his poll (see Chapter One). Just hang out with him for a few minutes. If he's relaxed and accepting, untie him and maybe hand-graze him for a little while as a reward. The next time, increase the amount of time he's tied and continue to be nearby. After he's pretty calm about this experience when you're around, go out of sight, but keep an eye on him. If he begins to show signs of getting upset, return and rub a couple of his favorite places. When he calms down, try it again. If he's quieter this time, come back and make a big deal of him and end for the day. In this way, he'll gradually accept tying for longer and longer periods with minimum fuss.

Next, I add a little bit of commotion and really begin to add patience to his lessons. The second place I like to tie is in a little higher traffic area. I continue to use a quick-release knot. I tie him, back away a little distance, then return and pet him. As before, increase the difficulty of this

3.4 A tree makes a good tying post—it won't break. Tie the rope just above the horse's head and give him a little slack. Always tie with a quick-release knot.

training "question" in small increments. Never tie him to, or with anything, that can break if he blows up.

The third place I tie to is a tree, the horse trailer, or to my ring, with a lot of horses going past (figs. 3.4 and 3.5). Make sure he has plenty of room on his tie, but not so long he can get a foot over it, or so high that you really have him stretched up. It should be a safe spot for him to stand while the world goes by.

You want him to wait calmly. At a rodeo, or a cutting event, all of the horses are standing around, tied up and waiting. Waiting is a big part of a horse's life, so he has to learn to accept it.

I used to work with a trainer named Hank Aldrich. Hank would take all the yearlings and tie them everywhere. In fact, if you drove a new car to his place, Hank was liable to tie a horse to each door of your car. When you got back to

3.5 Tie in various areas, like the trailer, to get him used to a variety of experiences. Notice the full leg protection for his safety.

your car, the horses would be chewing all of the paint off!

A horse that is bonded with another horse to an excessive degree, benefits from patience training. He discovers security and confidence in himself by being tied out. If you skip this step and go right to riding him, the horse will still be calling to his best buddy, and you might as well forget about training him. He won't be listening to you. He just wants to go back to his buddy. Tying out really does a lot for this problem.

Grooming

If your horse hasn't already been introduced to the grooming process, take this opportunity to develop your physical bond with him and teach him that it's pleasant to be handled. Begin in an area where he's comfortable, like his stall if he's used to one. Introduce him to the various brushes and curries slowly and pay attention to his reactions. The idea is to make this a non-threatening process and to keep the first introductions as positive as possible. Horses should enjoy a good grooming, but be aware that some horses are more sensitive than others. Watch for the red and green lights. If a firm stroke of a stiff brush is greeted with pinned ears, use lighter pressure. Experiment with fast or slow, and short or long brush strokes to find the tempo and pressure that relaxes him and creates green lights.

There will probably come a day when you bring a mud-caked horse in need of some elbow grease from the corral. If you set him up now to enjoy, or at least tolerate, grooming, he'll accept more pressure later if he's had a good roll in the mud. For now, prove that you have his best interests at heart by discovering his favorite places and respecting his "no-fly" zones. Encourage him to relax into the experience and to anticipate grooming time with pleasure.

This is also a good time to teach him to give you his feet when asked. Every farrier he comes in contact with throughout his life will appreciate this lesson. Find a signal you'll use every time that means "Pick it up." Most farriers use a pinch above the fetlock. Focus initially on getting the response of a lifted foot. Make sure your appreciation for the right response is loud and clear. Move in steps toward getting him to allow you to hold the foot, then to be comfortable while you hold the hoof and pick it out. Be sure you set him up to succeed by giving him the chance to keep his balance as you move from foot to foot. It's normal and necessary for him to shift his feet to support himself on the three feet remaining on the ground. Let him build up to perfect balance over time. This is a good lesson for him in other ways besides maintaining his foot hygiene. It gets him used to you moving around him and develops trust between both of you. It also keeps you attuned to his legs and how they are doing.

This is also a convenient time to put on his training boots. Front boots are indispensable; hind boots may or may not be needed, depending on the horse. Every horse in training should be wearing appropriate shin boots; add bell boots and/or skid boots as needed. When dealing with valuable horses, prevention is worth every cent that the boots cost. After you spend weeks treating a splint or have to stop training because of an injury, you will gladly put on boots every time the horse leaves his stall.

There are protective leg boots for every purpose, made of every type of material, including fabric and leather. The neoprene boots made by Professional's Choice work particularly well. The sports medicine boots made by this company seem to help horses in training, particularly those with an underlying problem. These boots feature a strap that goes under the pastern to offer additional support.

Bell boots are also necessary on some horses. Many young horses overreach as they refine their balance. One vet bill will buy a lot of $40 protective boots.

After using boots and other equipment, remember to rinse the sweat off, disinfect, and lay them upside down to dry in the sun to kill any bacteria. (You should also do this with saddle blankets and pads, laundering them periodically as needed.) If you are not careful about cleanliness, you can easily spread a fungus or other skin affliction to every horse in your string just by using contaminated pads, shin boots, or other gear. It's a good idea to have enough equipment so that every horse has his own, or enough to let you rotate from set to set so that there is always a clean set available.

Clipping

Getting a horse accustomed to being clipped should be an easy process if he was imprinted during the first three days of his life. Imprinting is a process of exposing a foal to lots of handling and stimuli so he accepts and chooses to cooperate with a human from birth. This process minimizes the trauma of handling later and builds bonds of trust that last a foal a lifetime. You can run the clippers around the foal and let him get used to the noise from the beginning. It will make your job much easier later on when it's time to give him a haircut. If this wasn't done at birth, you can make up for it by using RESISTANCE FREE techniques and common sense.

Don't come out five minutes before the show and expect to clip your horse. Instead, expect to devote at least an entire morning to the training process, using the **Pizza Theory** and **Patterning** as you work toward acceptance.

With a young horse, begin this exposure to clippers in a small confined area like a stall. He shouldn't be tied tightly. When you first turn on the clippers, stand out in front of the horse so that he can see and hear them as they are turned on. Move them around, up and down, but don't threaten the horse with them. Stay at a distance until he's used to them. Remember, don't use direct eye contact, as that is threatening to the colt.

The worst possible thing is to thrust the clippers right at the horse's face and demand that he get used to them, or else. If he begins to show fear, or backs up when you begin to approach, turn your back to the horse and turn the clippers

off to use Patterning to approach and retreat, and thus turn a negative into a positive. Take a couple of steps away, turn the clippers back on, and repeat. As soon as red lights of resistance appear, turn around again, shut the clippers off, and retreat a couple of steps.

This approach also illustrates the Pizza Theory. The colt learns to accept these scary monsters a little at a time and allows you to bring the clippers closer and closer. If he's pretty sensible and you are using good body language, this stage usually takes only a few minutes.

If the horse won't even allow you within 15 feet in the first few minutes, you will be spending several days in this training process. Don't use a twitch or other restraint on the horse, or you may be doing so for the rest of his life. Instead, take the time *now* to teach him to accept them. Don't force him.

The next step is to rub the buzzing clippers up and down his shoulder and neck. Don't worry about actually clipping him the first day. It's enough if you can just lay the clippers on his neck and rub them up and down. You can also rub them under his chin and on his poll. The next day is soon enough to start doing his bridle path, or fetlocks. Take all the time you need, and when resistance appears, turn off the clippers and back down for a moment.

The first time I clip a colt, I put cotton in his ears. This achieves three things. While putting cotton down inside of his ears, naturally you have to handle them, and this process desensitizes the ears. He then becomes more likely to accept the clippers when you approach his ears with them. Cotton also keeps the cut hairs out of his ears, as well as muffling the sound.

The ultimate goal is to be able to drop his halter rope and be able to clip his bridle path, chin, muzzle, ears, fetlocks, and coronet bands on the second day of clipper-training. With a difficult horse, it may take five clippings to work up to this point. But a young horse takes a few minutes to go through a process that can take hours or days with a spoiled horse. This is a strong argument for doing it right when he is young.

The abused horse that has always worn a twitch or a war bridle for clipping is an entirely different story. It may take ten days to get to actually clipping. Keep using the Pizza Theory and Patterning, taking small steps forward and retreating when necessary. I remember working with an abused horse that actually went through a wall when the clippers were turned on. He had to get away because he was terrified. It isn't meanness, it's fear.

Begin by setting up a horse like this with history for success. Choose a confined, safe area, and don't tie the horse tight. Select a small set of clippers and turn them on and off from 10 or 15 feet away, over and over. When the horse snorts and shows fear, turn them off and rub his body with your hand. When you actually begin touching his body with the clippers, start at the shoulder. It may take two days to get to the point of being able to rub the clippers on his shoulder.

Many horses can't stand the tickle of the clippers. Before clipping his ears or bridle path, rub these areas while holding the operating clipper. Let him feel the vibration and hear the noise. If the horse demonstrates resistance when you put the clippers in position to use, take them away and return to Patterning. Look at progress in terms of inches instead of feet.

I like to put my hand between the clipper and the ear at first. The hand absorbs some of the noise and vibration that would otherwise disturb the horse. On a real problem horse, I do some groundwork first to get into his mind so that he is listening and watching me, not tuning me out. Be very forgiving with the problem horse. You may not know what's happened to him.

Let the Old Teach the Young

The more I'm around other trainers, including dog trainers, the more I believe that horses and other domestic animals absolutely do learn from their peers and the youngster learns from the adult. You often see dog trainers tether young working dogs, such as sheepdogs and bird dogs, where they can watch older dogs work. As we've seen, tying a young horse in the ring while other horses are being worked can teach him about patience and accepting the realities of the working life. When horses get the opportunity to watch older horses work and be handled, they really learn trust and acceptance.

When I was in Europe I saw this approach used constantly. Harness trainers particularly believe in the power of letting seasoned horses introduce lessons to the young. Since a young horse can take courage from a solid, older horse, some driving horses are broken to harness in pairs, hitching a youngster beside an old pro who has seen it all. Some drivers go so far as to tie a youngster to the back of a vehicle during early training, letting him see and hear all the noise and activity up close, but in a safe situation.

The inexperienced horse can also learn from his elders when he's hauled to a show, or when he's tied around the training pens, without stress on him. Many ropers and cutters tie their young stock around the shows and rodeos to introduce them to the hubbub of competition. By the time these horses are actually competing, the charged atmosphere and noises are "old hat."

Futurity trainers take advantage of this principle as well. Futurity entrants cannot be shown officially before the futurity, but they can be hauled to schooling shows and events to be ridden around the grounds during competitions. The futurity horse learns from this exposure to mentally accept what's going on. He can do turnbacks or be worked in the warm-up ring free from the stress and demands of the showring and get a feel for the whole experience.

If you have access to a solid citizen to use as a "pony horse," he will be a genuine asset as you train the young horse. As you'll see in Part Two of this book, I recommend using an experienced horse a lot when teaching the young horse. Taking advantage of the younger horse's instinct to follow a more seasoned leader will increase the odds that you can introduce more and more new experiences without resistance, both in groundwork and as you get him used to the reality of working under saddle. In the upcoming chapters, I'll make suggestions for how you can successfully use older horses throughout the Four Phases of RESISTANCE FREE training to teach your youngster by example.

RESISTANCE FREE training is all about communication. Keep the lines open.

PART 2

Four Phases
of Training

Now we'll start applying some of the principles you learned in Part One as we get basic training with your horse underway. Remember to always let your horse tell you when he's ready for the next lesson in his RESISTANCE FREE education. At the end of each chapter, you'll find a step-by-step lesson plan to help you set up your RESISTANCE FREE training routines for maximum effectiveness.

During Phase One, you begin to establish leadership with work in the training pen. Rely on **Preparatory Commands** to teach the horse to trust and work with you. At this stage, you start getting into the horse's mind through control of his movement, direction, and speed with your body language. The Twelve-Step Program On The Ground that I introduce in this phase also emphasizes using Preparatory Commands to improve rhythm and timing between you and your horse. This program centers on emphasizing your leadership through moving the horse's shoulders and hips to increase his obedience and his focus on you, and as a bonus, his suppleness. Ground exercises designed to introduce your horse to the idea of responding softly to pressure on the halter and on his body follow. You'll complete Phase One with an introduction to work on the longe line, which provides more opportunities for reinforcing your mental control of the horse while you increase his obedience on the ground.

In Phase Two, you continue to emphasize groundwork (as you will in each stage of training). This phase introduces the next steps of the Twelve-Step Groundwork Program to continue building obedience and suppleness. If you have a quiet "pony horse" available, this is the time to get your horse acquainted with the idea of sharing his space alongside another horse. I describe in detail how to make ponying a positive experience. Also in this phase, you saddle and bit the horse for the first time. I take you through the process of selecting the appropriate tack and help you introduce it to the horse in a way he can easily accept. You'll find lots of information on preparing the horse to carry a rider for the first time (coming up in Phase Three), including techniques for improving his balance and flexibility.

In Phase Three, you introduce him to long lining. This work teaches the horse about forward movement and stopping in obedience to rein and voice aids, without the weight of a rider. When he's showing that he's confident in the work he's done so far, you can add a rider, using that reliable "pony horse" again to give him confidence. You'll stay at the walk and introduce stops and turns, encouraging him with Preparatory Commands and a balanced position to stay relaxed and responsive. Then reintroduce—this time under saddle—the first half of the Twelve-Step Program you did on the ground to begin to build on the lessons in rhythm and timing.

During Phase Four, you continue building obedience with this brand new saddle horse.

We'll finish the *under-saddle* version of the Twelve-Step Program, These exercises on two tracks improve the horse's responsiveness, flexibility, and coordination as he learns to use his front end and hindquarters at the same time in response to your leg and rein aids. Next, you introduce circles at the walk and trot. Your focus will be to develop truly round circles to promote balance and a good bend in the horse. When this work is done correctly, the horse develops confidence and trust in you. Another way to develop balance—yours and his—and to supple his shoulders in the process, is the Shoulder-Move Drill. This exercise refines the timing of your aids, too. "Doubling" is another exercise we use to teach Western horses about rebalancing their weight onto their hindquarters in order to execute a 180-degree turn. I'll show you how to set this exercise up using a barrier—a fence, for instance—and explain each step. Then we begin developing the lope (or canter) and finish our work with exercises for picking up correct leads. By the end of Phase Four, you and your horse will have laid the sturdy foundation on which you can build a rewarding partnership in whatever sport or discipline is in your future—Resistance Free.

Provide strong, sensitive leadership, sensible guidelines, and consistency as you proceed through your horse's basic training. Always make it your goal to encourage the softness that keeps your horse interested in learning what you have to teach. You'll find that the confidence and proficiency that result from your patience and attention to your horse's comfort zones are powerful bonuses of training with kind communication, knowledge, and awareness.

CHAPTER 4

Phase One:
RESISTANCE FREE
Training Exercises

LET TRAINING BEGIN!

You've decided that your horse is ready, willing and able, both mentally and physically, to proceed with his training. The initial groundwork in Phase One is just as appropriate for really young horses who still have some maturing to do before going on to saddle training, as you'll see in some of the photos that illustrate this chapter. Now it's time to begin the groundwork that will introduce the valuable qualities of steadiness and consistency to your horse's education enabling him to become a confident riding partner. Remember that you are totally responsible for the outcome of your training journey. Take pride in what you achieve together.

These lessons will set the stage for transforming your beginner into a performance horse. The Four Phases will result in some big changes in your horse's life, some perhaps more welcome than others, from his point of view. After all, he may have been perfectly happy playing with his buddies and cropping grass all day. Entering into this new partnership can become just as rewarding for him, though, if he enjoys his work with you.

Always remember: it takes what it takes to train a horse. Each horse is an individual. There is no set schedule for completing the Four Phases. Make your plans for each session and then be flexible about your goals based on the realities of each day. Be pleased with any progress, however small. Use positive reinforcement to tell your horse he's on the right track and watch your horse's motivation to work with you blossom like a flower. When you've gone through each step of this program, your horse will have a strong RESISTANCE FREE foundation in the basics. With solid training basics under your belt, every refinement you add later will be supported by the good work that came first.

"Read" Your Horse

As I learned from wild horses, every time you control a horse's space by making him move part of his body, you control his mind. This is an important principle of effective training, so I'll say it again so it's fresh in your mind. The horse who controls the other horse's space is the one in charge. When it comes to groundwork or riding, the trainer has to be the one in charge.

IN A NUTSHELL...

 Be sure the horse understands Phase One before you add the more challenging lessons from Phase Two, and so on through the Four Phases.

 Remember Richard's Rule Number 7 from Chapter One: "Avoid senseless repetition of a drill or exercise." When your horse has understood the question and responded appropriately, tell him you appreciate his efforts, give him a break and end the lesson, or go on to something else. It's not repetition that teaches the horse. Horses learn by routine, but drilling him over and over on the same thing makes a horse sour and unhappy. Establish and repeat a routine until he responds quietly, softly, and willingly, then quit. Endless repetition won't make him a better horse.

3 If you are smart enough to quit on a good note, the next day's training will be easier. If he's really easy to work with on Tuesday, then you did a good job on Monday.

4 Always think of any resistance you encounter as a powerful training tool. Your horse is telling you with red lights that it's time to take a minute to quiet down and relax. So step back, watch, and listen for clues.

5 Successful Resistance Free trainers focus on decoding the message the horse sends through his body language. If he communicates with resistance, your primary goal is to build trust so you get back to the green lights that mean the horse is ready to follow your lead again.

Over the years I've found that one of the most valuable things I share with the people who come to my clinics is a step-by-step series of drills and exercises that allow them to become leaders and take control of their horse's mind and body as soon as they walk into his stall. I know these exercises will work just as well for you. Before we begin actually working with your horse, here are a couple points on how to be the kind of leader your horse will choose to follow.

Use the information the horse gives you when you enter his space to begin to figure out the best approach for reaching your goal of establishing respectful leadership. Horses' reactions vary when you enter their space. I refer to this space as a **"bubble"** around them. Some horses will let you enter the bubble, put your hand three inches from their noses, and show no negative

response. Others will show tenseness and be protective of their space. Your goal is to prove you're no threat.

So, first enter the stall and, as I mentioned earlier, introduce yourself by letting the horse smell the back of your hand. I learned from Chief Rojas, a pioneering equine dentist in California with a huge amount of horse sense, that there is a lot more scent on the back of the hand than on the palm. Horses greet each other by scent. The key to making this work is to let the horse come to you and sniff your hand.

After you offer your hand, rub him in front of the withers, and watch for those green-light responses of head dropping, chewing, deep breathing, and a relaxed tail.

Be very conscious of how strongly your attitude and reactions can influence the horse's attitudes and reactions. Quick-moving people who work with sensitive horses can provoke a storm of activity without meaning to. You have to be able to literally slow yourself down into a Jell-O mode to get along with that nervous horse. After all, speaking as a person, if you're working with a hyper co-worker, you yourself may become a nervous wreck. Now this may generate a lot of productivity out of you, but it will be stressful! On the other hand, if you're relaxed and enjoying a nice break with a co-worker, not much else will happen for a while...but you'll be *so* laid back.

Relating this to horses, the quick-moving trainer will always get the most out of lazy horses, but will set nervous horses on edge. The quiet trainer will get along very well with hyper horses, but when coupled with a lazy type may find that very little is happening. That pairing may only get about a 60 percent performance as opposed to a 90 percent result. A versatile trainer will be able to switch mental and physical gears to work with both types of horses and get a lot out of each.

"Read" your horse constantly as you begin to train and adjust your attitude and lessons to meet his needs. Remember the principles of RESISTANCE FREE training I outlined in Chapter One. Allow your horse to choose to be obedient, apply pressure within the boundaries of his comfort zone for maximum learning, and look for the relaxation that means he's tuned in and ready to learn.

Make a Plan

Throughout all horse training, always plan your day, and then work your plan. Whether you scribble out ideas on your breakfast napkin or draft training programs on your computer, think about what you are going to do ahead of time. List what you hope to accomplish that day.

At night, sit down with a piece of paper and figure out what you could have done differently that would have made the training go five percent better. Actually, you can apply this to a broader application than just horse training! We'll consider it, however, in respect to your horses.

Remember that five percent isn't very much. That isn't even a major mistake. It's just small things that might have improved the training session, like quitting a little sooner, going more slowly through the drills, or getting the horse a bit softer. Maybe you feel you could have been better coordinated with your feet, or that your temper might have got the best of you at some point. Was the equipment adjusted as well as it could have been? Maybe the halter could have been fitted better.

Getting your plans and your improvements down in writing will make an amazing difference in the productivity of your days. Writing down your ideas for making the day five percent better will help curb you from making the same little mistakes you made yesterday all over again.

Organization can help you focus on what is important. Otherwise it's very easy to get so many things going in your life that you can't keep up with any of them. It's like trying to fill a teacup using a five-gallon bucket. The teacup doesn't really fill very well, and a lot of water gets wasted. Think of the water as your efforts during the day, and you'll see what I mean.

Now get your horse groomed and put his halter and boots on. Let's head for the training pen.

A good horseman takes more than a little of the blame and a little smaller share of the credit.

TRAINING PEN BASICS

The training pen, round or square, is a great tool for establishing mental control and putting you at the top of the **pecking order.** You'll learn a lot about reading and responding to each other's body

4.1 Begin work by letting the horse say hello quietly.

language in a pure way. Work in the training pen gives the horse total mental freedom, which is why I prefer to do this work without a halter.

After your horse has some experience with grooming and tying, he's ready to begin work in the training pen. If you don't have access to an enclosed pen, you can achieve these fundamentals on the longe line (which I'll discuss later in this chapter), although the freedom that's possible in the pen makes the initial lessons in mental control (yours) and obedience (his) a bit easier. Even if you don't have a pen, read this section carefully so you understand the process, which will come in handy when you work on the longe line later.

Start by removing the halter and letting the horse settle in the pen. Offer your hand and say a quiet "hello" (fig. 4.1). If you're working with a "General horse" (see page 31), or alpha mare, you'll see this horse mark out territory by dropping his head to smell the ground and then remain in that area. This instinct is important to notice and understand. The best way to establish mental control right off the bat is to move him from his chosen space. So advance quickly with raised hands and quick steps to drive him out of his territory. From the start, this establishes you as the leader.

Once you've shown that you control *his* territory, begin to pay close attention to his body language, which will give you the clues you need to reinforce your mental control of the horse through control of his body. If your horse responds to you with red lights—looking off as if you weren't there, raising his head, or bolting in

4.2 Use the whip in the right hand to "close the door." Advance with quick steps as you drive him from the rear toward the open door to the left.

flight—your response will be to drive him to the perimeter of the pen, controlling his space until the green lights of obedience come on.

You aren't trying to wear the horse out. You know he can keep it up longer than you can. Just keep him moving on the perimeter until you see an inside ear cock back to you or his head turn. If he lowers his head and neck, licks his lips, or takes a big breath, he is telling you, "Yes, you are the leader and I trust you." When he's given you these signs of confidence, slow your movement to slow his, until he's come to a stop. When you can stop him where you want anywhere in the pen and he then turns to you and comes over, giving up his space and entering yours, you have established mental control over his body and mind without ever touching him.

Until he readily relinquishes his space for yours, put him back on the perimeter and increase your requests that he move according to your signals. Advance quickly to speed up his pace, retreat to slow him down, and reverse his direction frequently. I use a long whip to "open and close doors" to the horse (fig. 4.2). For example, to move him right, I hold the whip out to the left to close that door and advance with quick steps toward his haunches to send him right. To reverse him, move in front to block that door and raise the whip. The more often you make it clear that you'll decide where he goes and how fast he'll get there, the more he realizes following your lead is the appropriate course. He'll soon flash the green lights you're looking for.

HERE'S A TRAINING-PEN ROUTINE I USE TO TEACH A HORSE THE BASICS OF BODY LANGUAGE SO I GET INTO HIS MIND

1 Settle the horse in the pen. (Start in a small 40-foot pen and later progress up to a 60-foot pen if you have access to one.) Read his body language. Watch to see if the horse establishes a territory. If so, quickly claim that space. Use raised arms and quick steps as you advance, applying pressure to move him out of his territory. Keep behind his withers for forward movement. When he cocks his head or ear to you, that's a green light.

4.3 For quicker movement, raise the whip and advance with quicker steps yourself.

2 Now ask for changes in speed and direction. Keep behind his withers for forward movement and control his speed with your speed (figs. 4.3 and 4.4). As you change direction with a nervous horse, breath out. Inhale deeply when changing direction with a lazy horse. To turn him into the rail, step toward his head. Step back and away to open the door and allow him to turn toward you. To teach the horse to face you while he reverses direction, stop his forward motion by moving into his path from a few feet away. If he is circling to the right, step back and raise the

4.4 To slow his movement, retreat, and slow your movements.

Resistance Free Training

4.5 *To reverse, step in front of him and raise the whip in your left hand to "close the door."*

whip in your left hand to block that exit. He'll then turn in toward you (fig. 4.5).

3 Watch for red or green lights right after you reverse him, change speeds, or make transitions between gaits. Base your next request on his obedience. Decrease the pressure if he's allowing you to make the decisions about where and when he moves. If the red lights are flashing, put him back on the perimeter and ask for frequent changes. Be alert for green lights and reward him by removing the pressure to keep going (figs. 4.6 and 4.7).

4.6 *Look for the "green lights": he'll turn and drop his head.*

4.7 *To speed his movement, raise the whip and drive him forward by moving toward his hip with quick steps.*

4 Teach him to stop: raise your hand and stop your feet. When he stops at your request, ask him to turn toward you and walk over to you. Draw him to you by backing away as you face him. Then turn, walk away, and let him follow you (fig. 4.8).

5 Your goal is to be able to reverse the horse toward you or away; stop him anywhere in the pen by stopping your own movement; switch from walk to trot or walk to lope whenever you ask for the transition; speed him up or slow him down by advancing or retreating yourself; and have him walk over into your space by drawing him to you. When he joins up to follow you without a halter or lead, you will know you have established mental control. This horse has become a willing partner (fig.4.9).

4.8 To stop him, move toward the horse's shoulder, raise your left hand, stop your feet, and say "Whoa."

4.9 Once he's joined up with you, always end the session with a happy horse whose expression shows he's glad to work with you.

BEGIN THE DRILLS

When you and your horse are ready to get started with three basic drills that follow, fit the halter correctly, with the crown piece in the poll groove, and pick up your seven-foot long, heavy, cotton lead rope. Before beginning this work in the stall or training pen, rub the horse right in front of his withers, where a mare nuzzles a foal. Use the palm of your hand in a circular motion going with the hair. You'll see the horse respond very quickly and become calm. As we saw in Chapter One, this type of human-to-horse contact creates a bond. The horse learns to trust you. Use it often in the process of training these exercises.

Remember to use **Preparatory Commands** as you work. I'll review the lesson from Chapter One: When you get ready to turn, turn your upper body in that direction before your feet begin to turn. This Preparatory Command is like a yellow traffic light that gives advance notice to the horse that a request for a new movement is coming up. It helps you create the leadership role and instills "follow me" in your horse.

The same applies when you get ready to stop. With your left hand holding the lead rope, raise your right hand before you actually stop and tuck your rear end underneath your body, just as you would to make a swing go higher. This movement gives the horse a yellow light to get ready. At first, apply downward pressure on the lead rope with your right elbow to cue the actual stop. Then lift the pressure in a quick release when the horse responds by stopping forward movement. Later on in the training progression, the Preparatory Command will just be to lean back slightly with your upper body.

To go forward, the Preparatory Command is to lean forward. First, make a very obvious upper body movement when working with a young horse. Within a couple of weeks, the movement becomes more and more subtle, and you can eventually do little more than nod your head forward and the horse will respond.

When you begin to school turns, turn your upper body in the direction you want to go with exaggerated movements to give the horse clear signals. Wait for him to learn, and be careful to adjust before he makes any mistakes. Eventually, a slight turn of your head will be enough to set him up for a turn. Remember, as I've said before, if the horse can respond to or see a fly, he can certainly notice you.

Use Preparatory Commands to teach your horse to relax and trust you. Your training will be more effective and require less time.

Begin these drills in your horse's stall.

The Sponge Drill

The Sponge Drill, the first exercise in RESISTANCE FREE training, is deceptively simple, and very effective.

1. Stand in front of the horse, about four feet away, facing him (fig. 4.10).

2. With either hand, squeeze the slack from the lead (as if you were squeezing water from a sponge) until he takes a step forward with the foot farthest from you. To do this he must shift his weight (rock) over onto the other shoulder. Keep squeezing the lead until the horse responds.

3. Then release the pressure by moving the lead slightly toward him. The pressure will also be released by the horse's step forward. Raise your hand to signal the end of your request for movement.

4. When he's got the basic concept, ask him to take three steps forward, then two, then one. Step back yourself to give him room to come toward you as necessary. Raise your hand to ask him to stop when he's taken the appropriate number of steps forward.

The Sponge Drill teaches the horse to yield to pressure on his face. He learns to give, not

4.10 The Sponge Drill. Squeeze the lead line as if you were squeezing water from a sponge to ask the horse to take three, two, then one step toward you. Raise your hand to signal him to stop when he's taken as many steps as you've requested.

resist. The more frequently he does this drill and the more quickly he learns to respond, the better prepared he'll be to accept later lessons and to yield to the bridle.

A horse usually responds very favorably to this drill because it is a language of give and take that he can understand. This exercise also teaches you how to use slack in the lead rope when training. If you pull too hard, the result is a jerk, and the horse will not react correctly. He loses his balance and rhythm when you use abrupt movements. Learn to be subtle with your cues.

This drill also teaches you the timing of the use of your hands. You learn to coordinate pressure and release. The hands must be used in sync with the horse's front feet. And, when riding, the rider's legs must be in rhythm with the hind feet. We call this keeping the horse between your hands and legs. The skill it takes to achieve this begins by coordinating hand and horse in the Sponge Drill.

I've taught thousands of people, and I have not met anyone who could not learn this drill in a matter of minutes and use it effectively. It's a great confidence builder.

The Independent Engagement Drill

The Independent Engagement Drill works like magic for both horse and trainer. The rider who gets the rhythm on the ground will find it instantly later when mounted. This drill will give you the beginnings of collection to slow and steady a horse. You can do it with a horse that wants to blow your hat off running down the rail and get him to where he can practically lope in his box stall! Done successfully, this ground drill will later lead to harmony of movement between horse and rider.

The Independent Engagement Drill is like dancing with your horse when it's done right and almost everyone in my clinics picks it up very quickly. It teaches the horse to cross his hind legs over as he does a turn on the forehand. The further he crosses over behind, the more engagement he will develop as he frees up his pelvis. Initially, this exercise may make him a little sore because horses aren't naturally accustomed to this movement, but the payoff is increased suppleness. You create engagement of the hindquarters, independent of the forehand.

This drill has been one of the methods I've used throughout my career to select some superstar horses. The ones who really step under in both directions with a good length of stride moving their hips are the true athletes. Those who step short or can't cross over behind are showing difficulty in mastering this movement and are less likely to perform well in the future.

1. For a circle to the left, hold the lead in your left hand, with the horse to your left. You will be inside the circle, as if you were the hub of a wheel (fig. 4.11).

2. Make sure the horse is focused on you, then begin to circle him to the left by taking the slack out of the lead as you rotate at the center of the circle.

3. As he moves forward around you, time the rise and fall of your feet to the steps of his hind feet to produce smoothness. This cadence between you and the horse connects your energies (fig. 4.12).

4. Once you have established a smooth forward circle, when his left hind foot (the inside hind, closest to you) lifts, squeeze the lead to bring his shoulders toward you and to activate that left hock (fig. 4.13).

5. He'll step more deeply from behind, with his hind legs on a separate track from his front legs. If necessary to keep his hindquarters on the second track, press and release with your right hand on his ribcage to encourage him to cross over behind.

6. His inside left hind leg will reach across in front of the right, suppling his pelvis, as he continues to circle around you.

7. As soon as he's given you three or four good crossover movements, stop and reward his efforts. (Increase the duration of this exercise gradually over the next few sessions to avoid making him sore.)

8. Change direction and circle him to the right, repeating Steps 1 to 7 in the new direction.

Remember this lesson from the training pen work as you do this drill: your body language affects the horse's responses. For a lazy horse, get crisper with your own movements, asking the horse to respond more energetically. On the other hand, calm a hot horse down by keeping yourself soft and quiet. The horse will pick up on your attitude and respond accordingly. Needless to say, never train in bad temper, or you'll go ten steps backward for every step forward.

To reward his honest attempts to cross over behind, rub him on the neck in front of the withers or behind his ears at the poll, which are two of the magic spots I've mentioned before. Remember to rub in a circle with the hair. I've watched a veterinarian take a horse with an extremely high pulse and cut it by nearly a third with circular rubs in those areas, going with the hair. I also watched him increase the pulse by a third when rubbing against the hair. Experiment with various fingertip and palm pressures to see which cause a lowered head or other green lights.

Another area to rub is just over the dock of the tail. I've watched wild horses grooming each other in this area. People who drive horses know about this spot. The horse's topline will really relax in response to a firm, circular rub right over the dock. Don't confuse this with scratching the horse, and don't rub against the hair. This is your key to bonding with the horse. You can actually see the green lights come on. When it comes to the horse's head dropping, it may get lower by only a half inch, so you have to pay attention. And when the horse's head turns toward you, it may only be two inches. Watch the ears and the expression in the eye. Chewing, and taking a deep breath, are definite green lights also.

4.11 to 4.13 The Independent Engagement Drill.

4.11 Begin to circle your horse to the left. You'll be at the center of the circle, like the hub of a wheel.

4.12 As he circles around you watch his hind feet and time the rise and fall of your feet to match his.

RESISTANCE FREE *Training*

4.13 Squeeze the lead to bring his shoulders in toward you. His left hind leg will cross over in front of the right as he circles. This movement supples his pelvis.

PROFIT AT LAST!

I taught a clinic in Scottsdale, Arizona, one year, and noticed a gentleman in his seventies who was there with his yearling. It turned out that the man's family had persuaded him to buy eight broodmares as a retirement investment. They envisioned horse breeding as a profitable enterprise. The end result was that he had eight mares and twelve young horses and the feed bill was sending him to the "poorhouse." He was seated on a bale of hay and the yearling was running frantically around him at the end of the lead line.

While at the clinic, this man came to realize that he needed mental control of his horses. He only learned one exercise—to teach the horse to walk beside his shoulder without having to hold onto the lead rope. He finally got to where he could do it without even a halter on the horse. He went home and taught all of his weanlings and yearlings this exercise. Four months later he called me and said, "This is great. I've just been working on this one thing, and it works so well. Once these horses trust you and build that bond, they are automatically sold. I've sold all of my weanlings and yearlings. I want to thank you. It's changed our whole life. Our feed bill has gone down and we're finally seeing some profit from all of this work. You can't believe how easy it is to sell horses when you don't have to rope them."

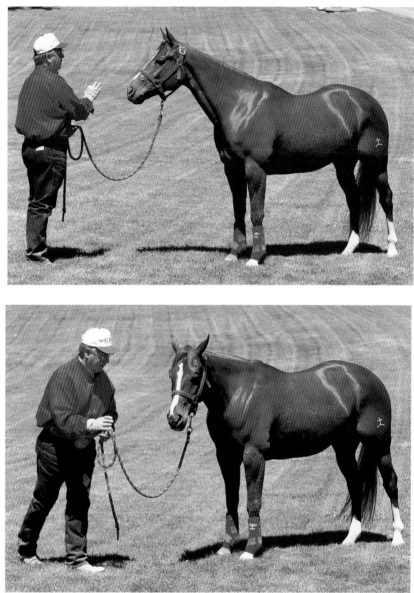

4.14 to 4.17
The Clock Drill.

4.14 Stand directly in front of the horse, with a loose lead. Raise your free hand to attract his attention.

4.15 Bend forward to pre-signal your intention, then turn three steps toward 9 o'clock. The horse should follow on a loose lead.

The Clock Drill

The Clock Drill is another useful drill to establish control of the horse's shoulders and body. There are a number of different positions you can stand in when working this drill with the horse. Think of the positions as 12 o'clock, 9 o'clock, 6 o'clock, and 3 o'clock.

My first goal is to control his shoulders. I stand directly in front of him, at 12 o'clock, about four feet away, then put the lead rope on my hip and slowly walk over to 9 o'clock (counterclockwise). The horse then has about four feet of slack to use in making his decision whether to follow or not (figs. 4.14 and 4.15). As I walk

4.16 Turn 90 degrees and take five or six steps toward 3 o'clock. Again, the horse should follow on a loose lead.

4.17 When the horse will do this drill with the lead draped over your hand, you've got ultimate lightness.

slowly to the new position, the rope gradually takes up slack and puts pressure on him, if he isn't coming along on his own. This draws his shoulders over to me.

Next, I move to the 3 o'clock position (fig. 4.16). The horse comes along, then I move back to 3 o'clock. I repeat this again and again, until the horse turns and faces me the moment I take a step. This is the first step in teaching the horse to work on a slack rope, and the first step in getting him to watch you for instructions, respect you, and give you his attention. When you can move back and forth from 3 to 9 o'clock with the lead rope never coming tight, you're making progress.

After about ten sessions of this exercise, the ultimate test is to just drape the lead rope around your hand and go through the drill with "no hands" (fig. 4.17).

The Join Up

Begin this exercise in good lead-line etiquette by walking the horse out of his stall. Walk boldly. Let him lead up beside your shoulder. If you lead him at an angle, as though you are afraid of him, your body language tells him, "You're controlling my space, and I want you to be in charge." Remember that your square shoulders and assertive step say to the colt, "I am the leader."

Walk ahead with authority. If the horse spooks, raises his head, or begins to back up, it's important not to reinforce any of these behaviors by turning to look back at him. Instead, keep walking straight ahead to give your horse confidence in you. Your body carriage and determination tell him that you are in control. Don't make sudden movements that would automatically reinforce his insecurities.

Ask the horse to stop by first turning your upper body toward him and then your feet, combined with a Preparatory Command: use your voice, or slow your feet as a pre-signal. A horse that responds to my stop command without my having to resort to pressure on the lead rope is giving me a bright green light. You are making good progress when you can stop him and walk on again without needing any pressure on the lead.

The next step is an advanced version of this exercise. It works very well for teaching the horse to follow the movement of your shoulders instead of responding to a cluck or other "go and whoa" cues. This work should be started in the round pen or other enclosed area.

Hold the lead rope in your left hand against your left hip. Bend your right elbow as if you are holding a flashlight and shining it forward in the direction you're going. As you walk forward, your motion will take slack out of the lead line and bring the horse along with you as he follows your right hand and square shoulders. When you stop, turn your toes toward the horse's shoulders. When you go, point your toes forward. Practice walking at different speeds, fast and slow, and encourage the horse to match you (figs. 4.18 to 4.21). The green light for this exercise is to be able to walk through an entire pattern as the horse follows your right hand and body language without any "rope" on the horse at all (figs. 4.22 to 4.26).

Synchronized Backing

The next exercise, synchronized backing, really controls the horse's face. Halt the horse with one front foot placed forward. Stand directly in front of him and face him. Don't get deep in his space and don't stare into his eyes. Ask him to back by pressing downward on the halter with the lead line as you step toward him. His automatic response will be to move the forward foot a step back. His moving back shows that you have just controlled his space. As the horse steps back, move with him, stepping toward him with your foot on the same side as the foot he moves back—like a waltz step.

Repeat the backing-up cue, asking for four or five steps at a time, always synchronizing your feet with his. He backs, you step forward. The ultimate goal is for both of you to move in perfect step. The horse will give you the green lights of dropping his head and chewing as signs of relaxation and obedience.

Ultimately you will be able to wrap the lead rope around the horse's neck and just point at the horse's foot with your foot—and he'll back

4.18 Hold your right arm and hand out in front. Lean forward as a pre-signal. Walk forward.

4.19 To lead him to the left, pre-signal by turning your body and right arm and hand out to the left.

4.20 To pre-signal a turn to the right, turn your body and right arm and hand to the right.

4.21 Do this exercise until it can be done without using the lead, using signals alone.

4.22 to 4.26 This series of five photos shows a balanced, rhythmic turn. The horse has joined up and follows in perfect step. This harmony comes from complete mental control of the horse.

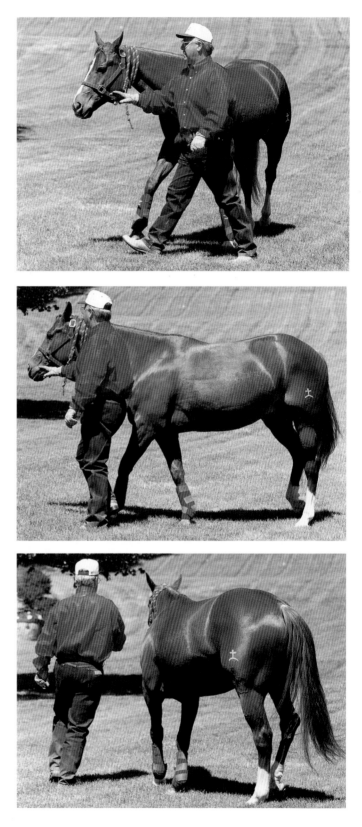

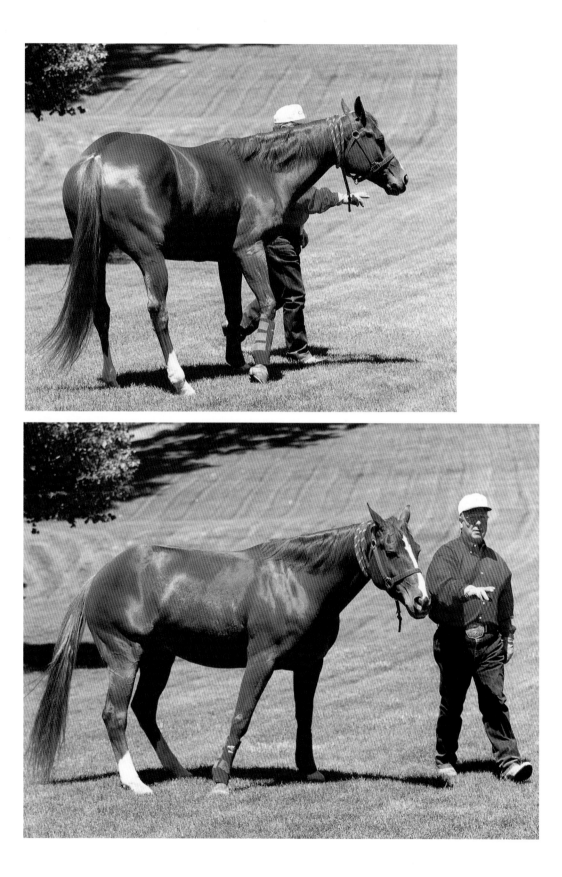

4.27 to 4.29 Synchronized Backing

4.27 (top left) Lead the horse between two ground poles placed at least six feet apart. The challenge is to back him out without hitting the poles.

4.28 (top right) As the horse succeeds and progresses, reduce the distance between the poles. This increases the challenge, requiring the horse to keep straighter.

4.29 (bottom right) As you back him, time your steps to match his.

RESISTANCE FREE Training

right up. You'll progress smoothly for several yards in perfect harmony because you have control of his body through his mind.

Once you've mastered this basic lesson, add ground poles as illustrated for a more challenging version (figs. 4.27 to 4.29).

The Square Drill

The Square Drill combines backing-up with a 90-degree turn. This drill frees up the shoulder and teaches the horse to shift his **center of gravity** back toward his hindquarters. Later in his training, this ability to shift his center of gravity will improve his ability to collect for more advanced work.

Begin the Square Drill by asking the horse to back four rhythmic steps. Next, signal him to shift his shoulders a quarter circle away from you—the first "corner" of the square. Watch that he crosses his inside foreleg over the outside foreleg to complete the movement. His hindquarters remain stationary as he pivots on the outside hind foot. Repeat this turn three more times to complete the square. As you progress, focus on completing the exercise smoothly, and in rhythm.

Let's start out by asking him to complete a square to the right.

1. Position yourself directly in front of the horse, facing him, with the lead in your left hand. Put about three feet of slack in the lead.

2. Back him four steps by stepping toward him (see the previous drill, Synchronized Backing) and stop. Move to his left shoulder. Press on his shoulder with your right hand to shift his front end a quarter of a circle to the right. Step forward as necessary so you remain close enough to continue to press and release while he shifts his shoulders away from the pressure of your hand.

3. His hindquarters should remain station-

ary as he shifts his weight back. He will pivot on his outside hind foot while he crosses his left front leg over the right to complete the quarter of a circle to the right. You have now finished one 90-degree corner of the square.

4. Reward his effort, then return to your position at his head, facing him. Ask the horse to repeat Steps 2 to 4 until he completes the square.

Repeat this drill in both directions until the horse crosses over in front, and uses his hind pivot foot smoothly.

The Circle Drill

The Circle Drill loosens the horse's rib cage and back.

1. Lead the horse from the side, with your shoulder lined up by his ears.

2. Walk a few steps and turn 360 degrees, with the horse on the outside of the turn. (This is just the opposite of the standard showmanship turn.)

If dealing with a sensitive horse make a circle of about six feet in diameter. With a lazy horse, make the turn smaller—as small and quick as possible. Encourage him to bend in his rib cage as he moves his shoulders and hips in a tight circle stretching and suppling his back and rib muscles.

The key to success in this drill is to use a lot of Preparatory Commands. Use your eyes and upper body to prepare the horse for this turn. Repeat this exercise with a few straight steps in between until the horse gives you a few green lights, such as chewing, dropping his head, or taking a deep breath.

Next, lay out four ground poles to form a square. The object of this drill is to have your horse complete a circle inside this square (figs. 4.30 to 4.37).

To really succeed in bonding the horse to you, make generous use of these schooling drills,

4.30 to 4.37 Circles in a Square

4.30 (Top) Use four 10-foot poles to make a square on the ground. First, encourage the horse to look at and smell the poles.

4.31 (Middle) Step into the square. Use smooth, rhythmic, RESISTANCE FREE steps to turn to the right.

4.32 (Bottom) Step in time with the horse's front feet and move his shoulders around the circle. The object is to complete a circle within the square.

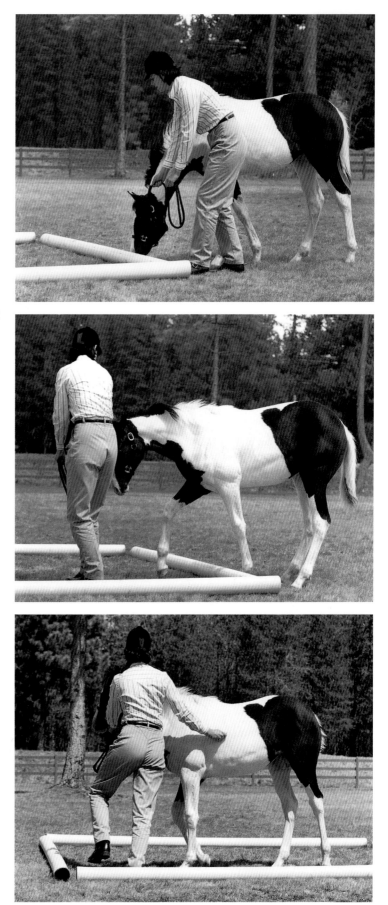

4.33 (Top) The horse achieves the objective and completes a circle within the square.

4.34 (Middle) When you complete the circle, maintain your rhythm and forward motion and lead the horse out of the square without stopping.

4.35 (Bottom) Come back into the square and head in the opposite direction. When going to the left, his back end will move around his front end.

4.36 Be encouraged by this horse's lowered head, a "green light." It results from your leading with soft, slow hands giving the horse confidence in your leadership.

4.37 After a clean, fluid circle, step out of the square from the opposite end.

including the Clock Drill and Join Up, and work without the halter. You should eventually be able to drape the lead rope around his neck and do all manners of turns and stops without any actual contact with the horse. When you have achieved this, you are clearly in your horse's mind. The goal is to obtain total mental obedience from the horse.

Remember to be consistent with your preparation before each training session. It places the horse in a good mind-set and opens him to learning. These drills confirm your ranking in the pecking order and make him more trainable. If you omit these drills, you never know what the horse's mood will be, and your training sessions will be like roller coasters, with lots of ups and downs.

Your later work under saddle can be more productive when you include these drills, because you will already have the horse's full attention. He will be more consistent during ridden training and ultimately in performing. Add the Twelve-Step Program to his routine next and begin to introduce him to the cues you'll rely on later when riding him.

INTRODUCING THE TWELVE-STEP PROGRAM ON THE GROUND

This set of ground exercises will begin to fine-tune your understanding of your horse's timing, rhythm, and responses to your cues, as well as teach him to move away from pressure. I call this the Twelve-Step Program. These basic lessons will be of tremendous value in your later work under saddle. I'll discuss Steps 1 to 4 here in this section, and address Steps 5 to 12 in Chapter Five.

The Twelve-Step Program requires obedience from your horse and will lead to more refined movement. As you control his hips and shoulders, you enhance your leadership role and communication with the horse. Remember, when you control his space, he goes into a "follow mode," which makes you the "boss horse." Also, each

maneuver sets the stage for the finer movements you'll need later for successful work on the trail, or for reining, or dressage. If you plan to enter the hunter/jumper disciplines with your horse, you'll discover that this foundation will give you the basic tools for lengthening and shortening strides before fences. This program also allows the horse to gain some concrete achievements on his way to becoming a confident saddle horse.

As a rider, you'll find that these exercises will increase your ability to synchronize your rhythm with those of your horse. Your timing will get better while you also build your horse's trust in your leadership. Later, your work on transitions, both on the ground and under saddle, will progress more easily, because smooth transitions are based on good timing.

To begin, put a halter and lead rope on your horse and find a fence line to work with.

Step 1: Hips Right

◆ Lead the horse from his near (left) side toward the fence. The lead rope is in your right hand (fig. 4.38).

◆ As you approach the fence, move the lead rope to your left hand, face your horse's barrel, and put enough pressure on the halter to shift his head a bit to the left, toward you.

◆ As he shifts, place your right hand against his rib cage in the area where your leg would cue him from the saddle. Now you're going to ask him to move his hips to the right a quarter turn by pressing your hand against his side. When each *hind* foot lifts from the ground, press. Release, when that foot reaches the ground. Apply pressure on the lead rope as each *front* foot leaves the ground and release when it is back on the ground. Time the movement of your own feet so you're in sync with his (fig. 4.39).

◆ Keep pressing and releasing until he stands parallel to the fence (fig. 4.40). Let him settle a minute, rub him in front of the withers, and walk him off.

4.38 to 4.43 Twelve-Step Program on the Ground—Steps 1 to 4

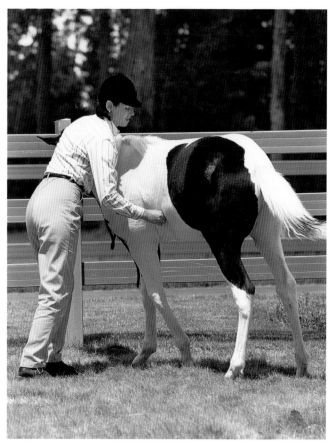

4.38 to 4.40 Hips Right at Walk, Step 1

4.38 Step 1a: Lead from the left toward the fence. Keep your shoulders square and your eyes forward.

4.39 Step 1b: Press with your right hand to move the hips over to the right, while his head comes toward you to the left.

4.40 Step 1c: Continue to use your right hand to move his hips to the right. The horse should finish this movement parallel to the fence, facing left. Step 2: Reverse aids for Hips Left at Walk.

4.41 to 4.43 Hips Left at Trot, Step 3

4.41 Step 3a: Trot to the fence line leading him from his right.

4.42 Step 3b: Press with your left hand to move his hips to the left. Move your feet in time with his feet as he moves his hips.

Step 2: Hips Left

◆ With the lead rope in your left hand, lead the horse from his off (right) side toward the fence.

◆ When you approach the fence, take the lead in your right hand. Face your horse's barrel, and apply pressure to the halter to signal him to move his head toward you to the right.

◆ As he begins to move, press your left hand against his barrel where your leg would cue him if you were in the saddle. Remember to press and release in time with his footfalls, as in Step 1.

◆ Turn the horse so he's parallel to the fence. Walk him off after a minute and let him know he did a good job.

Steps 3 and 4:

Repeat the above, but *trot* to the fence line, as illustrated (figs. 4.41 to 4.43). Really focus on the timing of your cues at this more intense pace.

4.43 Step 3c: The horse finishes the movement parallel to the fence facing right. Step 4: Reverse the aids for Hips Right at Trot.

Spend as much time as you need to master each step before continuing. Remember, if you need to drop back a step because your horse is having problems and showing red lights, do so. You're learning about his reactions and responses to your signals, and what you learn now will serve you well as his training continues. (For Steps 5 to 12, see p. 96).

LONGEING

Longeing is one of a horseman's most useful tools and is an important part of RESISTANCE FREE training. Longeing teaches a horse to move forward in regular rhythm. It also helps release the horse's tension and exuberance in preparation for training, while providing you with the chance to observe both his degree of focus and the quality of his movement on a particular day.

For work on the longe line, it isn't absolutely necessary to use a training pen. Although in many RESISTANCE FREE training lessons a training pen is a real asset, with skillful use of a longe line you can successfully establish mental control through body language while working in a larger, open area. The ground in the longeing area should be level and the footing good. In heavy footing, the horse will not be able to maintain his cadence. The area should be quiet, with a minimum of distractions. I like to longe in an area that has at least one corner to work with, perhaps a pasture, or a larger pen.

I like a longe line that you can tie some knots in to get some feel. A real lightweight longe line doesn't work well. It tends to float in the air instead of hanging down and giving contact. If you are using a standard longe line, choose the heaviest web or nylon one available. I also don't like using one with a chain, since it also makes it difficult to feel contact.

As for the horse's headgear, I prefer a halter to a longeing cavesson, which I don't find to have any significant advantages. I also often use a riata, which is a braided rawhide rope that

4.44 A rawhide riata half-hitched over the nose is more effective than it looks, keeping the horse's attention without requiring much pressure on the nose.

I loop around the horse's neck and then half-hitch over his nose to give me control (fig. 4.44). And of course, once you've introduced the horse to the bridle, which is coming up in Chapter Five, you can longe with it instead. Then, when you want to put some poll pressure into the training equation, you can run the longe line through the inside bit ring, over the poll, and fasten it to the outside bit ring. If a horse is getting a little "rowdy" with you, it really makes a difference in the amount of control you have when you fasten the line this way (figs. 4.45 and 4.46).

To longe him, first create a triangle with your arms. Walk to his right hip, extend your left arm with the longe whip, hold your right

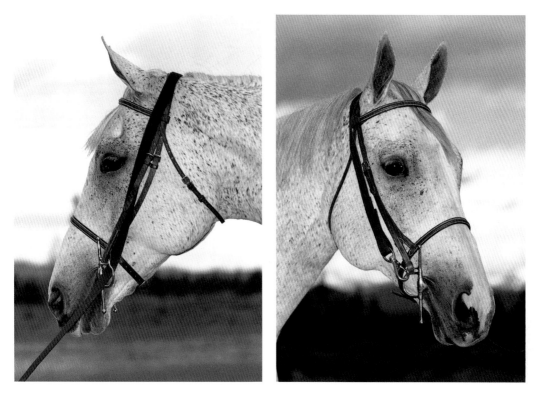

4.45 and 4.46 When the longe line is connected to the snaffle over the poll through the rings, pressure is applied to the poll and bit if the horse pulls.

hand out on the longe line, and the horse will go to the right. A longe whip helps keep the horse going forward (fig. 4.47). It should be long enough to allow you to make contact with the horse with the lash as necessary. You can add a length of baling twine to the lash end to give you more reach if necessary.

Walk in a small circle parallel to the one the horse is on, in time with the horse's walk. The rhythm in your feet is important because the similarity gives him security and reestablishes his rhythm if he loses it. It also helps your concentration. Focus on keeping your own rhythm steady, like a metronome. If you go fast, then slow, and sometimes stop, it sends confusing messages. Don't just automatically send the

horse out to the end of the longe line and expect him to be perfect. You must communicate with the horse using your body language—not just stand there in the middle like a statue. The sequence of photos (figs. 4.47 to 4.50) gives instructions for sending him out on the longe line and getting good changes of direction.

When ready to trot, raise your hand holding the longe whip, straighten your body, and quicken your step. Stomp your feet and signal him to go forward. Square your shoulders for more emphasis on the forward command. Now you are beginning to control his feet and build the horse's forward impulsion. If you want him to slow down, slow your motion, let the whip drop, and you'll see him respond.

4.47 to 4.50 Longeing

4.47 To direct the horse, close the door to the left by raising the whip toward his right hip. This opens the door to the right.

4.48 Keep your body to the rear of his withers and direct his movement and speed with your feet. Quick steps, and the raised whip, add forward motion to the lesson.

RESISTANCE FREE *Training*

4.49 To prepare for a change of direction, switch hands, lower the whip, and slow your steps.

4.50 To reverse direction, step in front of him and raise the whip to close the door to the right. Raise your left arm to direct him to the left.

Phase One: RESISTANCE FREE Training Exercises

91

TRAINING TIP:
WORKING WITH A LAZY HORSE

If you know your horse tends to be on the lazy side, your training work in Phase One can go a long way to improve his responses.

To motivate the lazy horse on the longe line, use a longe whip to reinforce your requests that he go forward. Strongly emphasize timing and rhythm in all your work with him, because if your aids are off, the lazy horse can really lean into your hand aids during ground exercises. Be prepared to use firm pressure to get a solid response from him during the drills and the Twelve-Step Groundwork Program. Your moves need to be quick and focused in these exercises. Keep your shoulders square, your chin up, and use assertive movements to cue him to respond crisply. In exercises that require you to move your feet, make your steps quick to encourage energetic movements on his part. Train this horse to succeed by ending a lesson when you see him make honest attempts to do as you ask.

Don't overschool a lazy horse, because this type will sour fast. Overwork can be a trap—don't fall into it. You won't change his nature by increasing your demands on him. Instead, work with his nature and set up your program so the horse always feels good about what he does. In the future when he's ready for sport-specific training, I recommend that you keep a lazy horse in a stall most of the time he's in training. That way, he'll be fresh when it's time to school him.

As far as I'm concerned, voice commands create rhythm as well as a good attitude if used properly. The voice also helps the trainer to stay quiet and focused. On the other hand, if a trainer gets loud and uses quick little words as commands, rather than long, steady, easy sounds, his voice reflects what he's really doing, which is challenging his horse to a duel. Your voice can make a radical change in the horse, so use it positively, to your advantage.

A definite red-light situation would be the horse that just takes off and runs without any heed to you or your commands. He just keeps speeding up and his head stays high in the air. When this happens, slow everything down and wait for him to come back to you. It doesn't do any good to get too excited at this point. Sometimes stopping him and backing him up a few steps is enough to get you back into his mind. (This would be a good time for the Clock Drill.) Change the focus of the lesson until you see green lights.

I change directions often in order to develop control of the horse's shoulders and hips. Pull him toward you and step out in front of him to make the change, using the sides of the training area to advantage if necessary. I work back and forth until I start reading some green lights in a horse's attitude. As soon as he begins dropping his head, or, when stopped, turns his head toward me, chews, or sighs, these are clues that the horse is understanding and accepting this new step in his education.

To stop when longeing, I may give the horse a verbal stop command, but I will also give a stop command with body language. I raise my right hand if he's going to the right, and left hand if he's going left, as well as stopping my feet movements. These Preparatory Commands are very important. I find that as soon as I can adjust my horse's rhythm with the movement of my own feet and can stop his feet at any time just by stopping my feet and raising my hand, it tells me I've finished the day's work. I don't like to longe the horse until he's hot and sweaty. Use the longe-line routine for getting "into his mind" and establishing control of him, then end the lesson.

I often see a person longeing a horse at a furious pace at a horse show or training barn, and then get on the horse and expect it to walk quietly. You can't bring the pot to a boil without it getting hot! The same goes for the horse. If you want a calm horse, work him calmly and quietly. The energy you create with your body goes right through the line to the horse. If you move quietly, so will he. If you're hyper, he'll pick that up, too. You cannot wear a horse out on the longe line. Many of our horses today have a lot of Thoroughbred in them, making them very sensitive and fiery. They don't wear out. Instead they get an attitude.

Some of the advantages of longeing are:

1. It's a great way to "read" your horse as you watch him move.

2. It gives you a chance to get "into his mind" and take control of his movements.

3. The longe whip provides an extended hand to encourage him to work around you developing forward motion, and indicates stops and turns.

4. It takes the "edge off" the horse before riding him.

5. It reinforces your mental control over the horse.

6. It sets up a good pattern of obedience on the ground before you mount.

As a trainer, it's up to you to prepare your horse to learn. You'll sometimes find he doesn't like being taught. That's normal.

Lesson Plan: Phase One

Here's the step-by-step plan I recommend for getting the most from the lessons in Phase One. Remember: accept responsibility for solid leadership, keep your horse cooperative and soft, read his red and green lights, channel his energies, and always include positive reinforcement. Let each small step carry you closer to your goals, even if it means going backward for a time.

Everyday is a journey toward the ultimate goal of a RESISTANCE FREE partnership with your horse. Each Phase may take a week or two, or a month or more. Remember: it takes what it takes. When your horse has done what you've asked, don't bore him by asking for the same move repeatedly. Repetition sideswipes your horse's desire to work for you. Show your appreciation and go on to another question, or give him a break. If you take pride in his progress, he will, too.

Step 1

Evaluate the horse. Watch him play and socialize to determine his position in the pecking order and observe his degree of coordination. Learn as much about him as possible.

Walk into his stall and observe his reaction. Groom, maybe do a little clipping, and put his halter on to see what his responses are. Lead and tie up the young horse, letting him get used to new experiences and learn patience.

Step 2

Groundwork in the stall and training pen begins. I perform the ground drills (p. 69) on a daily basis from this point forward, first emphasizing the movement of the shoulders, and later the hips.

In your work in the training pen, encourage the horse to be forward. Reverse directions at will. Teach the horse to stop when you stop your movement and raise your hands. Move your feet to cue faster or slower movement from him.

Each workout ends with a good cooling-out and grooming, which are as important as any other part of the training. The horse must go back to his stall in a relaxed state of mind.

Step 3

Continue refining the ground drills, as you will every day. Put the chain under his chin and lead him slowly and quickly. Work up to being able to use a lot of Preparatory Commands. This really begins to get you into your horse's mind and thinking about you. Move the horse's shoulders with a slack lead.

Step 4

During the ground drills, move the horse's shoulders and hips, and work your feet in time with his. In the pen, put the lead rope around the horse's neck and with him loose, go left, then right, while he follows along. Get more aggressive in the training pen with your feet and body Preparatory Commands and cue the horse to lope both ways. End by asking the horse to back up a couple of steps.

Step 5

Practice walking alongside the horse's shoulder with the lead rope up over his neck. Change direction with body language in the training pen. Back him up using your feet alone. Then continue through the drills and add Steps 1 to 4 of the Twelve-Step Program On the Ground (p. 85)

Step 6

Use this time to confirm any weak spots in the horse's schooling. Continue with the ground drills and developing rapport in the small training pen. Introduce the horse to basic longeing (p. 88). Work him lightly. It will take time to build his muscles, tendons, and ligaments for extended work on a circle. If you overdo today's introduction, tomorrow you may have a sore horse who resists the next lesson.

On the seventh day of training, turn the horse out to rest. Give him time to absorb the week's work.

CHAPTER 5

Phase Two: Groundwork to Prepare the Horse for a Rider

Let me say this once again: I believe you can't overdo groundwork. That's why I recommend that each phase of training includes groundwork to encourage steadiness and teach the horse about consistency. Groundwork also helps establish the horse's correct movement in both directions.

This phase of training prepares the horse for working with a rider later on in Phase Three. Because we'll start working on the horse's flexibility now, this is a good time to explain the terms "inside" and "outside" that you'll find used in many of the exercises coming up. As you'll see, in general, "inside" and "outside" refer to the direction of the bend of the horse's body when he works on a circle.

Let's say your horse is on the longe line in an arena, walking energetically on a circle around you in a clockwise direction (to the right), with the rail or fence to his left. In order for his hind feet to fall in the prints of his front feet on this curve to the right (this is known as "tracking"), his body will be slightly flexed to the "inside" of the bend—in this example, to his right. So, on a circle, the inside of the horse

is the side that contracts to allow him to flex around a curve. The horse's "outside" is the side of his body that stretches to allow the bend to the inside—in this example, his left side.

Because you change the direction of his bend when you change the horse's direction, you also change his inside and outside. So let's reverse the direction of the horse in our example. He is warmed up and trotting forward to the left now, in a counterclockwise direction. The rail is on his right side, now his outside, which is stretched to allow him to curve on the new circle. As he bends toward the inside of the arena, his left side contracts as he circles to the left. His shortened left side is now the inside.

The arena also has an "inside" and "outside." The direction toward the outer rail is always considered the outside of an arena. The direction away from the rail, facing the interior of the arena, is considered the inside. When you work in straight lines, with no bend, the horse's inside and outside will correspond to the inside and outside of the arena. For example, if you are using the rail while doing a ground exercise and your horse is facing to the right, with the rail on his left, his left side is his outside, while his right side, which is facing the interior of the arena, is his inside. The terms are also used in relation to the inside or outside of the arena when the horse is moving sideways without bend in lateral work. Remember that as soon as you introduce a bend, "inside" and "outside" will then be used in relation to the direction in which the horse is flexed.

Another important issue related to establishing correct movement in the horse in both directions is the fact that, like most people, most young horses are either right- or left-sided. I honestly feel this goes clear back to the foal's position in the womb. If the foal was curled to the left, he'll be shorter-muscled on the left side. If curled to the right, the short muscles will be on the right side.

In the majority of cases, the horse will favor one direction when turning and one lead whenever he is loping or cantering. Watch and see which direction he works in best during your sessions with him loose in the pen. For example, if the horse turns best to the left, that tells you his shorter muscles are on his left side and the longer, more flexible muscles are on his right side. His inborn curvature means he will bend more easily toward his shorter, more contracted muscled side, since the naturally longer muscles can do the work. The problem occurs when he has to bend in the opposite direction because the shorter muscles are the ones being asked to elongate.

As soon as you establish which is the less flexible side, begin balancing both sides in your training. Work him in his stiff direction about twice as long as his supple side at all gaits. This begins the process of equalizing the flexibility of the muscles on both sides of his body. Before we introduce the horse to the saddle and bridle, use the following exercises to help rebalance the naturally one-sided horse into a well-rounded athlete.

THE TWELVE-STEP PROGRAM ON THE GROUND (CONTINUED)

Remember, the Twelve-Step Program develops timing and communication between you and the horse, while improving lateral control and flexibility. It also prepares the horse to understand your cues to control and move his shoulders and hips later when you begin to ride him. I discussed Steps 1 to 4 in Chapter Four (p. 85). Let's go on.

Steps 5 to 8 are exercises that increase your horse's ability to use his hips and shoulders in a more independent way, while you both polish your timing skills. These skills will come in handy for jobs such as opening and closing gates and, later, establishing correct lead changes under saddle. Finally, Steps 9 to 12, develop the skills that prepare a horse to make smoother lead changes and cleaner circles. These exercises will refine your awareness of the horse's movement on your way to developing what I call "maximum feel." Work toward a progressively higher level of collection and straightness as you perfect these movements over time.

Step 5: Forehand Turn (Hips Right)

◆ Put the horse's halter and lead on and head back to your fence.

◆ Position him facing the fence. Stand at his shoulder on the left (near) side.

◆ Put your right hand on his left side, where your calf would give him a cue (fig. 5.1).

◆ To cue him to make a turn on his forehand, apply pressure on his barrel so he shifts his hindquarters to the right and pivots on his front legs. Apply pressure when he lifts his hind foot and release when it's on the ground. Use the lead to keep him from stepping forward. The fence will also discourage forward movement.

◆ Ask for a quarter turn. He'll be parallel to the fence. Go on to Step 6.

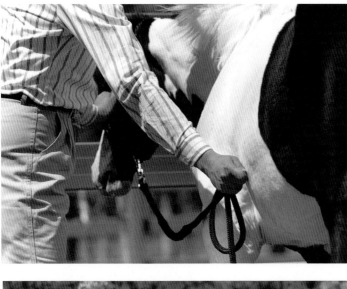

5.1 to 5.10 Twelve-Step Program on the Ground—Steps 5 to 12

5.1 Forehand Turn—Hips Right, Step 5: Press the ribcage with the right hand to move hindquarters to the right, with head bent to the left. Continue to move the horse to the fence.

5.2 Forehand Turn—Hips Left, Step 6: Once the horse is parallel to the fence use the opposite aids to move him back to where you started.

5.3 and 5.4 Haunches Turn—Shoulders Right, Step 7

5.3 Step 7a: In the Haunches Turn—Shoulders Right, his shoulders shift to the right. The right hind foot is the pivot foot. Note the left front leg crossing.

Step 6: Forehand Turn (Hips Left)

◆ Keep him parallel to the fence. Move to the off (right) side, take the lead in your right hand, and stand at his shoulder.

◆ Put your left hand on his barrel as in Step 5.

◆ Cue him to make a turn on the forehand by pressing his side in time with the steps of his hind feet as he shifts his hips to the left. Again, use the lead to keep his front end stationary (fig. 5.2).

◆ After a quarter turn, he'll be facing the fence.

Step 7: Haunches Turn (Shoulders Right)

◆ Face him away from the fence. Stand at his head on the left side.

◆ Cue the horse to move his shoulders to the right by applying pressure on the halter as he pivots on his hind feet. In the beginning, you might want to place your right hand on his left shoulder to help direct him to shift his shoulder (figs. 5.3 and 5.4).

◆ Turn him a quarter turn so he's parallel to the fence. Go on to Step 8.

5.4 Step 7b: Move your feet in time with the horse's feet.

Step 8: Haunches Turn (Shoulders Left)

◆ Face him away from the fence. Stand at his head on his right (off) side.

◆ Cue the horse to move his shoulders to the left by applying pressure on the halter in time with his steps as he pivots on his hind feet. As in Step 7, in the beginning, you might want to place your left hand on his right shoulder to help direct him to shift his shoulder (figs. 5.5 and 5.6).

◆ Turn him a quarter turn so he's parallel to the fence.

Step 9: Hip In

◆ Lead from the horse's left side along a fence line so you're at his shoulder, between the horse and the fence. Take the lead in your left hand.

◆ Place your right hand on the horse's left side where your calf would cue him from the saddle (fig. 5.7).

◆ Apply pressure to cue the horse to move his hips away from the fence and angle his body.

◆ Walk the horse for four or five strides with his hips away from the fence and his head toward the fence.

Twelve-Step Program on the Ground—
Steps 5 to 12 (cont.)

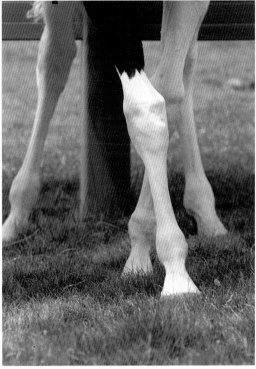

5.6 Step 8b: The right front leg crosses over and the left rear hind is the pivot foot.

5.5 and 5.6 Haunches Turn—Shoulders Left, Step 8

5.5 Step 8a: In the Haunches Turn—Shoulders Left, shift his shoulders to the left, using your right hand on his halter and your left on his shoulder.

5.7 Hip In, Step 9: Lead from the left and use your right hand to shift his hips to the right. Keep his shoulders left so that his left hind foot follows the track of the right front foot.

RESISTANCE FREE *Training*

- Then release the pressure and allow the horse to straighten for several strides along the fence.
- Repeat the maneuver no more than three or four times.

Step 10: Hip Out

- Lead from the horse's right side along a fence line so you're at his shoulder. The horse will be between you and the fence. Take the lead in your right hand.
- Place your left hand on the horse's right side where your calf would cue him from the saddle.
- Apply pressure to cue the horse to move his hips toward the fence and angle his body (figs 5.8 and 5.9).
- Walk the horse for four or five strides with his hips toward the fence and his head away from the fence.
- Then release the pressure and allow him to straighten for several strides, walking parallel to the fence.
- Repeat the maneuver no more than three or four times.

Step 11: Sidepass Left

- Stand on the horse's right side by his head.
- Place your left hand on his right rib cage in the area where you would cue him from the saddle.
- Apply pressure on the halter or lead rope to cue the horse to move his shoulders left (fig. 5.10). At the same time...
- Apply pressure with your left hand to cue him to move his hips to the left. As he steps to the left with his front feet, apply pressure on the halter or the lead rope. When he steps with his hind feet, apply pressure on his right side with your left hand. Move your feet in time with his.

- Sidepass your horse four or five steps or until he moves sideways with straight, balanced, fluid movement.

Step 12: Sidepass Right

- Stand on the horse's left side by his head.
- Place your right hand on his left rib cage where you would cue him from the saddle.
- Apply pressure on the halter (or lead rope if you have it in your left hand) to cue the horse to move his shoulders right. At the same time...
- Apply pressure with your right hand to cue him to move his hips to the right. As he steps to the right with his front feet, apply pressure to the right on the halter or lead rope. When he steps with his hind feet, apply pressure with your right hand. Move your feet in time with his.
- Sidepass your horse four or five steps, or until he moves sideways with straight, balanced, fluid movement.

If he has a problem with any of the Twelve Steps, avoid repeating the request. Instead, go back a Step or two, or an earlier lesson, walk him off for a few minutes to diffuse any frustration (yours or his), or go back to an earlier lesson so you can quit on a good note. Come back to the problem Step later on or the next day. Keep him in his comfort zone. That's where the potential for learning is at its maximum.

PONYING

Ponying is a good learning experience for any young horse. It gets him used to seeing a person over and above him and also helps him learn to accept the presence of another horse in his space. You can really see the difference in the young stock that gets ponied when you compare them with the ones who never got this training. The ponied horses are miles ahead of the others in handling intrusions in their space.

5.8 and 5.9 Hip Out, Step 10

5.8 Step 10a: With your left hand on the right ribcage, shift his hips toward the rail. Keep his shoulders off the rail with your right hand on the lead line.

5.9 Step 10b: From this rear view, you'll see that the horse's right hind foot should step into the same track as the left front foot.

If you've got access to a calm "pony horse," I really recommend that you take the time to use that experienced older horse to help teach your youngster by example. Always use a "pony horse" that's gentle and really broke. He should be good-natured. Older geldings are usually per-fect. Few stallions and mares will tolerate the banging and pulling inflicted on them by young horses.

The first week of ponying should take place in the training pen to keep the young horse out of trouble. On the first day, ask another person

5.10 Sidepass Left, Step 11: For the sidepass left, have the horse face the fence and move his hips with your left hand, and his shoulders with your right hand on the halter. Keeping shoulders and hips in a straight line is very important in this exercise. Step 12: Reverse the aids for Sidepass Right.

to ride the "pony horse" while you lead the young horse alongside (fig. 5.11). You'll discover where his comfort zone is while he's in close proximity to the older horse. Once he's nonchalant about this step, pass the lead line over to the rider. Next, progress to riding the "pony horse" yourself.

Take only a half wrap on the saddle horn, making sure to give the colt a little room. Only use a long cotton rope and don't tie tightly (fig. 5.12). I don't recommend using a chain. One way to start him calmly is to walk forward, keeping the colt between a sturdy fence and

you. This "chute" keeps him focused and forward. When he relaxes, reward him with a "rub." I like to reach down and rub the young horse's neck, poll, and back (fig. 5.13). Reach over him as often as you can. Make all of your movements very slow and quiet. Stay at the walk, so the experience is a nice, quiet one, for the first couple of days. Keep working in the safety of the training pen for the first ten days, or longer if you need to, and gradually introduce turns and transitions (figs. 5.14 and 5.15).

By the time ten days of ponying in the pen have passed, you should next be able to trot

5.11 to 5.16 Ponying

5.11 Always introduce ponying training with a ground helper and a good-natured, gentle "pony horse."

down the side of a road or through a pasture safely (fig. 5.16). Don't get in a hurry and head out before you've put that ten days into him. You don't want him to learn he can pull back, or jump, and get into trouble. If he gets away in the first ten days, you're safe in the enclosed area and you aren't looking at an expensive colt on his way to becoming a "hood ornament."

1. Ponying gets a horse used to seeing a person above him.

2. Ponying takes the edge off a fresh young horse.

3. Ponying teaches a young horse to accept other horses in his space as he is bumped and moved around.

4. The "pony horse" gives a young horse confidence.

Keep your training goals high enough to be inspiring, but realistic enough to keep you encouraged.

FIRST SADDLING: EQUIPMENT

Your horse has come quite a distance in his education so far, and I hope you're feeling pretty optimistic about his future. Now we add a really important experience to this horse's life. It's time for horse and saddle to meet. This

5.12 To begin with I use a half loop around the horn. Leave the horse 24 to 30 inches of rope.

5.13 To calm the colt and reassure him that movement above him is no big deal, rub his neck. Also pet him to reward him when he relaxes.

Ponying (cont.)

5.14 and 5.15 Use the training pen or other small area to begin, if you can. At first, ride your "pony horse" making turns to the right, into the colt. Continue to rub his neck to calm him.

5.16 Once you've built trust and confidence, pony in fields and along roads to expose the young horse to many new experiences.

is a lesson you really want to go perfectly. Think about how many thousands of times you'll want to saddle your horse in the coming years. If this first introduction goes smoothly, it's likely that you'll avoid a bad experience down the road. So think this one through and take the time to make it a really positive experience. Start with evaluating your tack.

As I said before, any equipment has to fit well, be adjusted correctly, and be in good condition. Be sure you select and adjust your gear so that it works as it was intended. If the horse isn't comfortable, he won't be concentrating on what you have to teach him. No matter how good a trainer you are and how good a horse you have, if your gear isn't right, you won't get very far at all without some problem, big or small, derailing your hard work.

Keep your equipment maintained properly. If it shows wear, fix or replace it. Equipment failures are dangerous, they can interrupt your training, usually at the worst possible moment, and may upset your horse, giving him a permanent bad memory that's going to take a lot of work to fix. Certainly he will be a little unnerved, at the least, if the girth breaks and you go flying over his shoulder.

Use a saddle that is not too heavy—a synthetic or lighter **stock** saddle, or an English type, for first-saddling purposes. You can never have too many rings on one! Surprisingly, some people select older saddles with broken trees to use, on the theory that it won't matter if the horse damages an old saddle. This is one of the worst choices you can make, because a broken saddle will make a horse's back sore and give him a reason to stop learning and look for any way out. Chances are, however, your horse will easily accept the RESISTANCE FREE saddling experience and won't do the saddle any harm anyway.

Check saddle fit constantly throughout the training process. A colt may start out mutton withered and develop a nice set of withers after a few months under saddle. This will likely change his saddle and pad requirements. Keep in mind that if any equipment does not fit or causes soreness, it can be like you having to walk twenty miles with a pebble in your shoe—uncomfortable at best and damaging at worst. Pain sure isn't going to help you build a good relationship with your horse. All he's going to want is for you to stop and go away. And worse, a saddle that doesn't fit can damage the muscles in his back and his withers—sometimes permanently.

Bad saddle fit can also be the cause of behavior that looks like resistance. If your young horse gets sore and doesn't want to work under saddle, especially if he's done well with the training to date, suspect your saddle. Consult an experienced horseman to assess the saddle fit, or talk to a professional saddler about whether your saddle can be customized to fit your horse's back. It may be time to replace the saddle for one that matches your horse's conformation better.

Thick, fuzzy pads cause a saddle to be unstable which can make a horse nervous. I consider them to be of no use. Felt pads or blankets, such as the Navajo blanket, actually grip the back. The Navajo can't be beaten for performance and quality. The horse's back is kept cooler by the natural wool fibers. In contrast, the synthetic polyester pads don't breathe and can be dangerous to ride in because they are slippery. Avoid them.

Introduce the Saddle: Patterning

I like to begin the process of introducing the horse to the saddle in either the stall or pen,

PATTERNING

While Patterning him, watch his ears. They are just like antennae, showing you where his attention is. Watch the level of his head. If he raises it, that's a red light. If he drops it, you've got a green light. Read his tail. A clamped tail is a red light. A relaxed tail is a green light. You want all lights green before you continue with Patterning. Wait till his head is low, his ears are soft but listening, and his tail and topline are relaxed. The horse should be standing quietly. Until the horse can stand quietly and he chooses to stick around as you work around him with the saddle and blanket, you aren't ready to progress with this introduction.

using a method that I call "**Patterning**." As we saw when we brought in the clippers in Chapter Three, the process of Patterning turns a negative into a positive and changes **red lights** into **green lights**. You can avoid creating bad memories that last a lifetime when you use Patterning to teach a horse to accept new things in his life. Compare the benefits of this quiet, gradual approach to the process of sacking out.

In the old way of sacking out, the trainer generally tied the horse or hobbled him to restrict his freedom, walked up to him, and basically assaulted him with an item, slapping the horse all over with the blanket or whatever. Eventually the horse just surrendered. This slam-bam process made for a spooky horse. He couldn't get away from the frightening object and the urge to flee stayed trapped in his mind. That's why the sacking out process destroys a horse's trust.

As I always say, if you want to be trusted, be trustworthy. A wise trainer gives the horse the

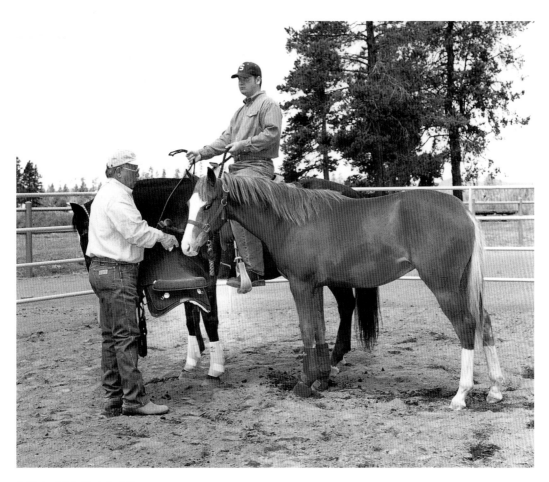

5.17 to 5.26 First Saddling

5.17 In the pen, use a "pony horse" for added confidence. As in the stall, let the young horse check out the saddle and wait for "green lights."

option to leave. Otherwise, even into his old age, he will still be a nervous horse. When you work in the training pen or his stall, he is free but really can't go far, and he can still express his opinion. This avoids that long-lasting sense of being trapped that makes him less than reliable later on in stressful situations. Remember, horses are prey animals and the instinct to flee danger is built in. This is one reason that Patterning is the better way to introduce new experiences. The Patterning approach keeps the horse's options open and allows him to take as much time as he needs to accept that you aren't approaching him with a horse-eating monster, after all.

Another disadvantage to sacking out is that while you might get the horse used to a sack, a blanket, or a newspaper—there's always something new coming down the "pike." You have to

First Saddling (cont.)

5.18 If you do get a "red light"—a raised head, here—just turn and walk off.

continually add on to the sacking process. With Patterning, once he learns to trust that the blanket or saddle isn't going to "bite" him, he draws reassurance from your positive feedback and remembers the good outcome. You'll find that Patterning does work. Although it may take more time at first, in the long run it builds a quieter, gentler, and more trusting horse.

Here's how I use Patterning to help a young horse to accept tack. In figures 5.17 through

5.19, the "pony horse" has joined us in the pen to give the young horse added confidence and security as I begin to introduce him to the saddle. (Remember to Pattern both the blanket and the saddle—this horse in the photos was introduced to the blanket earlier.) I slowly approach the horse with the saddle, keeping my eyes lowered and unchallenging (fig. 5.17). As soon as the horse begins to show red lights—in this case, he's raised his head—I stop, turn my back, and walk

5.19 When you're back to "green lights," settle the saddle into the cradle of the horse's back.

away (fig. 18). Once he's settled after a moment or two, I walk back up to him with the saddle. I may get a foot closer before he begins to show me red lights. Eventually he accepts the presence of the saddle in his space, looks at it, and bonds with it. Once he realizes that this new experience did him no harm, suspicion and fear melt away.

Keep approaching and retreating as necessary until you can walk right up to him. Let him smell the saddle. Once you've got consistent green lights as you bring the saddle closer to him, lift it up near his shoulder. When he accepts that position, place the saddle lightly on the horse's back and wait for him to settle. When he meets this new sensation with green lights, move the saddle around on his back (fig. 5.19). If you get a red light, just walk off and come back when he's quiet. Then shift the saddle around until he accepts the sensation and gives you green lights.

BASIC SADDLE PATTERNING INSIDE

Working in a stall may be the best idea with a horse that is easily distracted by outdoor activity. It's also a good place to make progress in his education if the weather isn't cooperating. Figures 5.20 through 5.22 , demonstrate the basic saddle patterning process in a stall, with a horse who has previously accepted the saddle blanket. In figure 5.20, notice the slack lead rope and relaxed expression as this horse drops his head to explore the strange item that's in the stall with him.

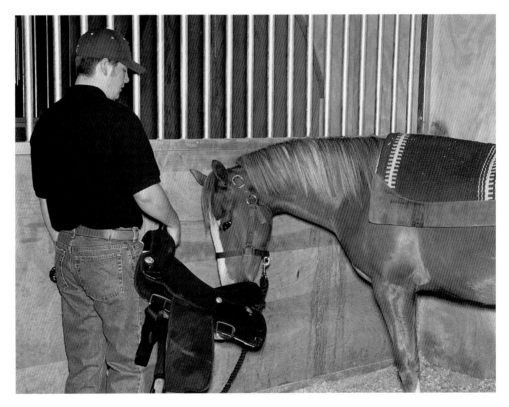

First Saddling (cont.)

5.20 In the stall, give the horse time to check out the saddle and build trust.

5.21 Move slowly and watch the horse's ears, nose, and eyes for continuing "green lights." Stay close to him and place the saddle lightly on the back.

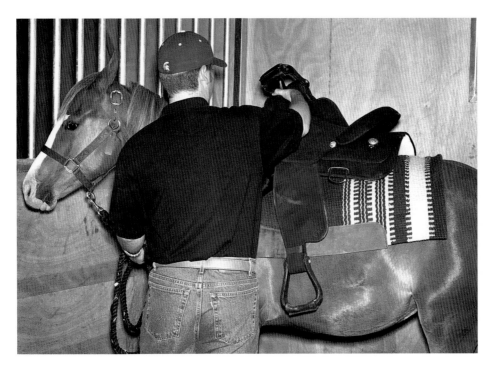

5.22 Move the saddle back and forth and around and watch for "green lights" before you cinch.

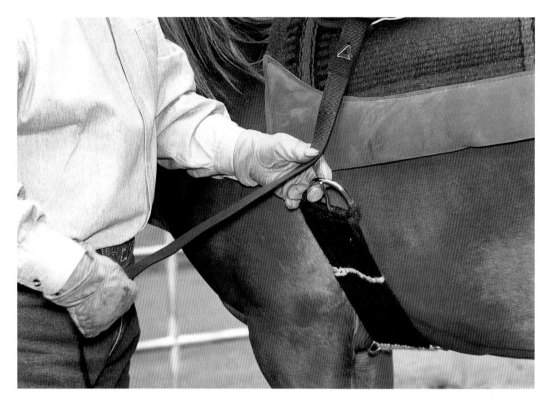

First Saddling (cont.)

5.23 Always keep the cinch right next to the belly as you tighten it up.

The next step is to repeat patterning from his off side to prepare the horse for accepting the saddle being placed on his back from either side. Remember that what you do on the left side must also be done on the right side. What they see out of the left side is entirely different from what they see on the right. So always Pattern both sides. When he's nonchalant about placing the saddle on his back from both sides, remove the saddle and give him a break. Tomorrow you can add the experience of a tightened girth.

In the training pen on the following day, repeat the Patterning process as necessary—in the reassuring presence of the pony horse, if you can—until the horse again quietly accepts both the blanket and saddle. Now it's time to fasten the cinch for the first time. Before you do, let the pony rider take the lead line. Slowly take up the girth with the fingers of your left hand and hold it up around him snugly for a few minutes (fig. 5.23) This teaches the horse to accept the feeling of something wrapped around his middle before you try actually fastening the cinch. If he's claustrophobic, you're going to find out right here. If the young horse reacts strongly to the fastened cinch, just allow him to circle the pony horse and settle down (fig. 5.24). Provide lots of reinforcement when he's quiet (fig. 5.25). Then let the rider walk him around quietly for a few minutes to get him accustomed to these new sensations (fig. 5.26). Your goal is to build as much trust as possible into this experience. So take your time and let him tell you when it's okay to take the next step forward in his training.

5.24 If the horse blows up in response to this new sensation, just let him circle the pony horse and quiet down.

5.25 Rub the horse continually to calm and reassure him.

First Saddling (cont.)

5.26 Spend some time just walking the horse in the safety of the training pen.

A BIT ABOUT BITS

I prefer to start horses in **snaffle bits**, in part because they will be expected to show in bits later in their careers as senior horses. Also, horses are very responsive to the snaffle, and you can achieve much greater refinement than with the hackamore or side pull. A trainer with quiet hands can get a better feel for the horse's rhythm with a bit, and get a little more "finish" in a snaffle. The advantage of a snaffle lies in the direct connection from your fingers to the horse's lips. As the horse chews, the sensitive rider feels every motion. The snaffle bit also gives superb lateral

control of the shoulders, while suppling the poll. The horse enjoys relative freedom of his head while you introduce him to the leg aids. This freedom allows the horse to be more mentally relaxed and accepting of training.

The best snaffle for starting the young horse is a large, smoothly tapered variety. This bit is very forgiving to the horse. The thicker the mouthpiece, the milder the bit. The larger diameter mouthpieces spread the pressure over a wider area in the mouth. In contrast, thin bits concentrate their impact and are less comfortable to the sensitive, uneducated mouth.

D-ring snaffle

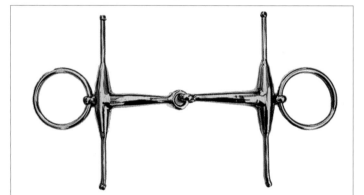

Full-cheek snaffle

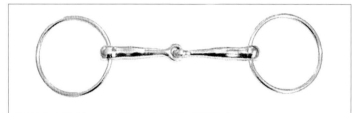

O-ring (loose ring) snaffle

Eggbutt snaffle

5.27 to 5.32 First Bridling

5.27 A selection of snaffle bits. I prefer the full-cheek snaffle, but the others are also useful and suit some horses very well.

Do not use any bit with a rough mouthpiece, such as a chain, wire, or twist, when starting a young horse. Even a slow twist will "bite" the colt and make him reluctant to accept the bit. The young horse's mind is just like a computer. If you load in bad experiences, you'll get bad results. If you put in computer chips that say "hurt" and "fear," you'll have a horse that is nervous and uncomfortable. We want him to accept the bit as something that will forgive him and communicate with him and not be a source of pain.

To illustrate how this works, press a pencil across the palm of your hand. If it is one of the pencils with multiple flat sides, you'll feel what a slow twist bit is like. Now find a larger, round pencil, the kind they give to first-graders, and press that against your palm. There is a noticeable difference, isn't there? Now imagine what it would be like to have a piece of wire wrapped around your palm and pulled hard. That would be a very different feeling. The horse's mouth is far more sensitive than your hand, and it must be treated with respect.

I like to start with a smooth, tapered full-cheek ring snaffle with a fairly thick mouthpiece. This is probably one of the most forgiving bits you can use. The taper of the broken snaffle bit naturally distributes your signals to the lips of the horse. I prefer the full-cheek snaffle because of its balance and the way it helps bring the horse around in turns. A D-ring, or eggbutt, snaffle is another fixed-ring bit and has a similar effect to the full-cheek snaffle. An O-ring, or loose-ring, snaffle is carried differently by the horse. Because the bit isn't fixed to the rings, the horse wants to pick up and hold the O-ring. Whichever version you choose, the snaffle rings or cheeks should be large enough so that the bit cannot be pulled through the mouth (fig. 5.27).

Choose a bit that the horse likes. Stainless steel bits are durable and widely available. The silver alloy bits are very appealing to the horse because of their taste. A sweet-iron bit is also well accepted. Rubber should be avoided because

horses generally don't like the taste. Aluminum and chrome-plated bits should also be avoided; aluminum dries the mouth and chrome flakes off, leaving a rough surface. There are enough choices that you can find something to suit every horse. Obviously a trainer needs to have a wide selection of bits on hand.

INTRODUCING THE BRIDLE

I recommend choosing a bridle with a browband. The browband keeps the headstall stable, which allows the bit to sit evenly in the horse's mouth. It is important that you initially adjust the bridle so the bit forms two to three wrinkles in the corners of the mouth. This does two things: it automatically insures that the horse will never get his tongue over the bit, and it keeps the movement of the bit to a minimum, which avoids frustration. The horse's mind is fresh and open at this stage. If he never gets his tongue over the bit during the first 20 rides, he will never try again. However, if he succeeds during that time, he will have the tendency to try and get his tongue over the bit whenever there's a little pressure on him. But only keep the bit snug for the first week to ten days. Later on, lower the bit to one to two wrinkles in the corners of his mouth. As long as he does not learn to put his tongue over the bit in the first place, your horse will generally be content to leave it in the correct position.

The reins you use in training should be heavy and at least seven feet long. I like the braided parachute cord reins. Their weight allows you to get a feel of the horse's mouth and to communicate with him using a slack rein. You can also use leather reins. Seven-foot long training reins provide plenty of length for "checking" (also known as "bitting") a horse, or doing a little long-lining (I'll talk about checking and long-lining later in this chapter).

If you use a Western bridle, always attach your reins to the bit with screws, ties, or another solid method of attachment, *not* metal snaps

5.28 To prepare him for the bit, use soft fingers to rub his lips, gums, and tongue. Allow him to lick and chew without resistance.

5.29 Let the bit come into light contact with the horse's lips. (By the way, I prefer to remove the reins when bridling for the first time).

First Bridling (cont.)

5.30 Use your fingers to open his mouth and pull the headstall up with your right hand.

5.31 Slowly adjust the bridle over one ear at a time.

RESISTANCE FREE *Training*

5.32 Check to make sure you've got two to three wrinkles at the corners of his mouth and that everything is adjusted properly.

that vibrate the mouthpiece and send false signals to the horse. You don't want any signals between you except the ones *you* send.

Before actually placing the bit into the horse's mouth, use your thumb and forefinger (which are naturally soft and at body temperature) to rub his lips, gums, and tongue (fig 5.28). Your goal is to desensitize the area and prepare the horse for the feel of the bit. Get the horse to lick a little. Also make sure that he has no sharp points on his teeth, or wolf teeth, that will interfere with his acceptance of the bit. Some horses

need dental work before going into training. A horse that is uncomfortable in his mouth is not going to accept the bit properly.

In preparation for placing the bit in the horse's mouth for the first time, remove the reins from the headstall. It is a good idea to put sugar or sweetener on the bit before you put it in his mouth. When the horse is ready, put the bridle on slowly, one ear at a time (figs. 5.29 to 5.32), and encourage the horse again to lick a little. Nine times out of ten the horse will accept the bit immediately.

CASE STUDY: ZIP'S ALLIGATOR

Zip's Alligator is a four-year-old stud colt being shown in Western Pleasure. He's a good mover, but when the rider takes hold of the reins in a class, this horse responds by gaping (opening his mouth) and champing the bit, especially when the circle is reversed for the final phase of a class. When Zip's Alligator lines up at the end, the gaping and champing increase. This is behavior that he never displays in the schooling ring at home. The key to this puzzle is pressure: mental and physical.

In his everyday training, this horse appears to tolerate this particular bit. But when the added dimension of show tension increases the degree of mental pressure he experiences, it overloads his ability to cope with both the show ring tension and the uncomfortable pressure in his mouth. His evasive response in the ring tells me that it's likely that the process of introducing the bit during this horse's early training went too quickly or that the bit is too severe for this horse's level of training—maybe both. If he were wearing the correct bit, he would not respond to show ring pressure this way. The bit is definitely the problem, and the solution is to back up, reevaluate the horse's training, and find him a more suitable bit.

This talented young horse's case is proof that you can never take too much time in the beginning. Don't steal a ride by going quickly to a severe bit and then fool yourself that he is responsive and light because of your great talent as a trainer. Pretty soon, holes will appear that prove you cheated both yourself and the horse.

I usually give the horse some time to get used to the bridle without any saddle on his back. You may want to turn him loose in a pen to let him further his acquaintance with the bridle and bit. Make sure the reins are removed and be sure there are no nails or projections anywhere in the pen where he could snag the bridle or bit, and get hurt or damage the equipment. Many a nice horse has had his mouth ruined just because somebody's gone to the house and forgotten to keep an eye on him. If the horse gets caught on something and pulls back, you have a really bad situation. Keep him in sight while he's adjusting to the experience.

I allow about ten days to let the horse get thoroughly used to the bridle. Many people get too hurried at this stage. They want to get the bit in and go. I remember when I was a youngster, my dad did that frequently. He would grab my brother or me by the seat of our pants and throw us in the middle of a young horse and watch the fireworks. The horse would take off and we would save our lives by pulling back on the reins and bruising the horse's mouth. Don't risk bad memories and a damaged mouth. Take this step slowly. I work him in the training pen or longe him with the bridle on during this introductory period, watching to see that the horse is moving forward and becoming better balanced as his lessons proceed.

THE CONNECTOR BIT

Traditionally in the education of Western performance horses, as we refined the horse's ability to work **in the bridle** in a balanced way we progress from the snaffle, to the hackamore, and then to a **curb bit**. (See the sidebar, *Toward Making a Bridle Horse*, for basic introduction to this progression.) Today, many all-around horses do both English and Western classes. That's one reason the traditional middle stage, hackamore training, is used less frequently these days. Also, the hackamore can be expensive and difficult to adjust correctly. So I have developed a new bit called the Connector Bit (see Resources). This bit has worked for thousands of Western riders and their horses making the transition between snaffle and curb without the hackamore.

Hunter-jumper riders have also found this bit to be a valuable tool for establishing better responses from horses that tend to lean on the bit or ignore the rein aids. It lightens the horse's forehand without the need to resort to a curb. For the same reason, it has also been an effective choice for older horses that just don't respect a snaffle. So whether your Western horse is progressing in his education, or your older horse needs help reestablishing his balance and respect for the bit, the Connector Bit may be a good choice.

The Connector Bit has a swept-back shank to keep the horse from grabbing it with his lips and works like an elevator bit, providing pressure straight down on the lips with no leverage effect at all. This bit has no curb strap, so it doesn't grab like the curb bit can. The mouthpiece has a round connector ring, like a sucker, similar to the design of a French link, which is a three-piece snaffle with a flat plate in the middle that encourages the horse to pick the bit up. The round ring in the Connector Bit

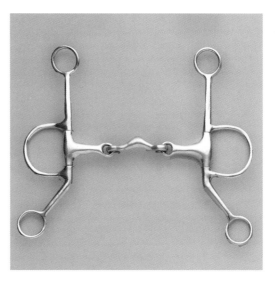

5.33 I developed this bit, called the Connector Bit, to help Western riders make the transition between the snaffle and the curb bit. It allows for the continued familiar action of the snaffle with the addition of a new mild curb-like action from a second rein attached to the lower shank ring.

gives some tongue and palate pressure. Because it's smooth, you have more control with less pull (fig. 5.33).

Another feature of this snaffle is a tapering mouthpiece, which gives the horse tongue release. Since various muscles attach and connect the horse's tongue all the way to the sternum, tongue release frees up his front end. This helps a horse shift his **center of gravity** back so that his hindquarters more effectively generate the energy needed to keep his shoulders up.

A plus with this new bit is the way it hangs in the headstall, allowing you to give the horse reliable Preparatory Commands, primarily through poll pressure. Poll pressure releases endorphins to create a feeling of well-being, while also allowing you to pre-signal before your actual command comes through. The Connector Bit is a tool to create timing and rhythm between rider and horse and may be a better option for today's versatile horses.

TOWARD MAKING A BRIDLE HORSE

In the Four Phases of training presented in this book, I focus on the snaffle bridle to get your horse started on his journey soft and free of resistance. If your eventual goals for your horse include more advanced work in the Western disciplines or perhaps dressage, be aware that other headgear will be incorporated to refine your horse's sensitivity, obedience, and movement as he advances. Here's a very basic introduction to the complex subject of making a Western bridle horse.

If advanced work with your horse is now (or later becomes) a goal for you, learn as much as you can, take all the time you need, and work with a good instructor whenever you can. Your efforts will be worth it, because a horse trained to such a high level is a joy to ride and a pleasure to see.

As I said, different headgear than the plain bridle is used to develop advanced horses. In dressage, a horse is required to work in a double bridle when competing from Fourth Level on. A double bridle uses both a thin snaffle called a bridoon and a curb bit, each with a set of reins. An accomplished rider with an advanced horse can use these tools to refine flexion and create the sensitive communication that allows the horse to work in a balanced frame throughout complex patterns of movement. This blend of balance and collection is known as self-carriage. The advanced Western rider shares the goal of developing his horse's self-carriage. This process is known as "making a bridle horse." A Western bridle horse carries himself and his rider with balance, ultimate softness, and sensitivity, equivalent to a highly trained dressage horse. In developing a finished bridle horse, hackamore training plays a central role.

When a Western horse has advanced beyond the Four Phases of training presented here and he can

5.34 This mild, 3/4-inch hackamore is the best choice for beginning hackamore training. The wider nosepiece sends a clear signal to the nose, jaws, and poll.

achieve flying changes of lead and a soft, fluid counter-canter in the snaffle, he's ready for hackamore training. A hackamore works by applying pressure to the horse's nose, jaw, and poll, encouraging him to flex at the poll and really use his back and hindquarters. The three hackamores pictured here each serve the same basic purpose, but the "volumes" are different.

5.35 The 5/8-inch hackamore delivers a medium level of pressure to the nose, jaw, and poll, and is most popular for the second phase of hackamore training.

The 3/4-inch hackamore (fig. 5.34) is a good introduction. The wider nose piece provides a "louder" signal to the horse that his uneducated nose can "hear," without being harsh. Once the horse is responsive to a quiet signal from the wider, 3/4-inch nosepiece, introduce the 5/8-inch version (fig. 5.35). The goal is now for the horse to respond softly to the thinner nosepiece, which can send a sharper signal. The rider's hands need to be extremely controlled in order to use just enough pressure to get a response, and not an ounce more. The final stage of hackamore training is achieved with the pencil bosal (fig. 5.36). Of course, the thin nosepiece must be used sensitively to produce sensitivity in the horse.

Then the pencil bosal can be combined with a bridle and curb bit to help make the transition to the curb alone. Much like the double bridle used in upper-level dressage, the curb and pencil-bosal combination uses two sets of reins. This is known as "two-reining the horse into the bridle." The final stage in the making of a Western bridle horse is to use the bridle and curb bit alone, which brings the horse into complete self-carriage.

As is true in every stage of training your horse, from the basic lessons presented in this book through the finished bridle horse, the horse's gentle, soft obedience is a prerequisite to moving to the next stage. With that goal in mind, RESISTANCE FREE progression through the levels of horsemanship becomes a beautiful partnership between horse and rider.

5.36 The pencil bosal is appropriate for the third level of hackamore training. The finished horse responds with lightness to the thin nosepiece, which would be too severe for a less educated horse.

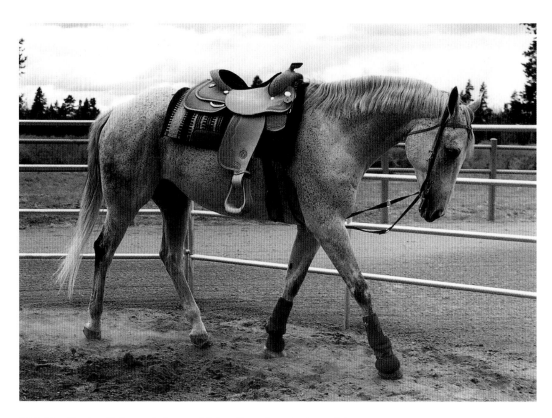

5.37 The Rhythm Collector helps establish self-carriage in the training pen.

THE RHYTHM COLLECTOR

When your horse goes forward with rhythmic motion while being longed in the bridle, we say he has developed longitudinal (forward to back) balance and flexion. This ability tells you he's ready for the process of "checking" (sometimes known as "bitting") that introduces the lateral flexion that teaches him about side-to-side balance. (I'll tell you how and why to "check" the horse a little later in this chapter.) The important qualities of forward movement and longitudinal balance necessary before you begin building lateral balance are also developed when you train your horse in a Rhythm Collector.

The Rhythm Collector is a training device I designed (see Resources) that helps enhance the horse's front-to-back balance (fig.5.37). I use it soon after the bridle is introduced because it is a great way to let the horse teach himself about giving to pressure. This simple tool teaches him to use his back and hindquarters effectively to power his movement as he shifts his center of gravity back. The Rhythm Collector is basically a very long rein or rope that uses poll pressure to help the horse learn to shift his center of gravity toward his engine—the hindquarters. As he lowers his head in response to the Rhythm Collector, he begins to use his back and hindquarters to propel from behind, rather

5.38 Later, use the Rhythm Collector under saddle. Notice the horse's relaxed expression, and the rhythmic give-and-take in the lines.

than pulling himself along on the forehand.

To use it, run one end of the line through the near bit ring, over his poll, and down through the other ring, so that the middle rests at his poll. Then pass the two loose ends down under his chest and up behind his elbows to his back. Either attach them to the D-rings on the saddle if you are working him in tack or secure the ends together behind the withers (fig. 5.38). Be sure he has enough slack to allow him to drop his nose.

On the first day in the Rhythm Collector, let the horse begin to figure out how to find his balance while he's loose in the training pen. Then add daily 20- to 30-minute training pen sessions for a week or so. Work at the walk and trot to start. Change his direction, ask him to stop moving and then move off again. What you'll look for is for him to respond to poll pressure by dropping his head, which also raises his back and puts his hindquarters well under his body. When you see him relax into this new balance, stop him and pet him—make a big deal out of him. When he can change gaits and directions smoothly, ask him to pick up the lope or canter. This gait really improves when he uses his back and hindquarters effectively, but be sure to build up the length of time spent at the lope gradually, so he doesn't get sour. Whenever he releases at the jaw and the poll in relaxation, praise him generously and let him walk or rest.

You can also use the Rhythm Collector while longeing. Thread the longe line through the inside bit ring, under his chin, and attach it to the outside ring. Don't use a chain. Watch for him to develop good rhythm and relaxation in all gaits. Keep longe-line sessions short and sweet as he develops **cadence** and muscle.

Later, the Rhythm Collector can help your horse to fine-tune his balance under a rider. He learns to soften his jaw in response to quiet pressure at the poll and on the corners of his mouth. In turn, this relaxation in his jaw influences his entire body, allowing him to reach through with his hind legs to more easily carry and balance both himself and you.

While the horse is moving strongly forward, the Rhythm Collector is absolutely consistent. It is simple to use, reliable, and will never set a horse back in training.

"CHECK" HIM OUT

Next, we want to introduce the lateral stretch your horse will need to balance himself and your weight. This stretch is called flexion and it allows him to strengthen his neck and poll so he can work from his hindquarters efficiently. A good way to begin this training is the process of "checking," (bitting) which I mentioned earlier.

Start this lesson in his stall. After saddling and bridling, use your seven-foot training reins for checking work. Check the horse to the right to encourage him to stretch the muscles on his left side. Tie the right rein to the right stirrup, just short enough to encourage the horse to bend slightly to the right. Tie the left rein to the stirrup long enough to allow this bend. Make this a very slight, gentle bend. Tie him like this for about eight to ten minutes.

Old-timers used to check the horse directly to the cinch ring, but this can make a horse *lean* on pressure instead of giving and taking. Using the stirrup to tie to, comes closer to duplicating the give-and-take action of your hand, and has a "live" feel to it. In contrast, the "dead" cinch ring is rigid and unforgiving. If you use a Western saddle, the stirrup provides "live" feedback to the horse equivalent to about four pounds of rein pressure. But, when I'm developing a horse that needs to be very sensitive to the rein aids—say, a reining horse—I use an English saddle for this work. Being checked to the lighter stirrup teaches the horse to carry himself and work with about a pound of pressure.

I pick up the stirrup that I've tied the rein to and hold it very lightly. I move it gently to encourage the horse to give at the poll and bend. This demonstrates to the horse what I'm looking for in this exercise, and he will learn to do it on his own much more quickly. He learns that he can release the pressure by giving in to it. Soon, any pressure at all causes him to yield. The exercise teaches the horse to give, or yield, to the bit in response to light pressure.

I've always found it interesting that when you check him on the left side, he has to learn all over again, to the right, so remember to teach the lesson on both sides. When he does yield, I rub him generously where he likes it. Then let him teach himself how this works in action by moving him quietly around the stall. When he gives to the pressure on the rein, praise him.

If the horse is right-sided, check him first to the left stirrup. Don't bring his nose all the way around—just bend his neck slightly—and don't overdo this exercise in either direction. The horse should spend twice as much time checked to his stiff side as he does on his good side so really observe him carefully in your ground work to discover which is his stiff side. For example, watch to see if he has trouble picking up the right lead, or bending to the right in a nice arc. If he does have difficulty check him to the right more frequently than the left, to begin to get him more flexible through his right side. After this basic preparation, the horse will bend more easily to the right when he's ridden.

After checking the horse to one side and then the other to establish lateral flexion, longe him in his tack, using the seven-foot long training reins evenly as side reins to help teach him about finding and working in the correct frame. This work teaches him to stay straight in the bridle while he accepts bit and rein pressure from fixed reins. This lesson differs from the Rhythm Collector, which applies poll pressure from reins that move in rhythm with the movements of his shoulders to teach the horse to balance. However, both tools can improve your horse's balance during forward motion.

When using a **stock** saddle, I run both reins through the stirrups and tie them over the seat of the saddle, up by the horn. In English tack, tie up the stirrups and run the reins through them and then fasten them up over the seat of the saddle (see fig. 6.5 in Chapter Six). Run the longe line through the inside ring of the bit, over the poll, and fasten it to the outside bit ring and then send him out on the circle.

At this point the horse is ready to learn more about balancing his body in a desirable frame. I like to see a horse flex at the poll, coming off the forehand with lifted shoulders as he begins to work more from behind. However, some horses will respond by leaning into the fixed side reins and getting heavier on the forehand. In that case, discontinue using them. Instead, rely on the Rhythm Collector to rebalance him. Even if the horse successfully finds his balance in the side reins, use them sparingly. Once the horse has found good balance off the forehand, he won't need side reins any longer.

On that note, I'll end Phase Two. In the next chapter, your horse will learn to apply his new balance as he begins to carry a rider.

*If good horsemen learn
from their mistakes, many
are getting a fantastic education!*

Lesson Plan: Phase Two

Continue ground drills in the stall and training pen on a daily basis. Emphasize backing-up and the timing of your feet in this work. Also continue with longeing and round pen work without a halter. Observe whether he is right- or left-sided.

Step 1

The last eight steps of the Twelve-Step Program On the Ground improve timing and lateral movements, so add these to your horse's list of accomplishments. If you've got a reliable "pony horse" on hand, introduce him to ponying. Lead your horse alongside the pony horse to begin this new experience. Once he's relaxed, let the pony rider take the lead rope and teach the young horse about sharing his space.

Step 2

Begin saddle and blanket Patterning in the training pen. The young horse learns to accept this equipment as part of his environment.

Step 3

The next day, saddle the horse in the presence of a reassuring older horse to build confidence. You may have to reaffirm some of yesterday's Patterning work. Carefully tighten the girth for the first time. Pony the young horse with the saddle for a short time. This ends the session for that day.

Step 4

Saddle the horse up and make sure he accepts the tightened girth, and then longe him in the saddle. After he works off some energy on the longe line, introduce him to the bridle for the first time, using a snaffle. Be sure that any wolf teeth are pulled before you take this step. Massage the horse's mouth with your fingers before you put on the bridle. Make much of him. Slip it off very carefully, and put it back on, repeating this about a dozen times until the horse is completely comfortable with the idea of being bridled.

Step 5

Let the horse wear the bridle (without reins) while longeing him in both directions. Remember to allow him about ten days to get accustomed to the bit. Confirm your previous work. Continue with the ponying lessons.

Step 6

Introduce him to free work in the pen using the Rhythm Collector. Then it is time to put reins on the bridle for the first time and "check" the horse in the stall to begin side-to-side flexion exercises. Start by flexing him away from his stiff direction. Let him stand for eight to ten minutes before you change him to the other side for four to five minutes. Rub the horse's poll while his head is flexed to encourage him to relax and learn about giving in to the pressure to relieve it.

Step 7

Next, longe in the round pen using both reins as side reins. Make the reins equal length so the horse's head is straight.

Let him have one day off in seven to rest and process his new lessons.

CHAPTER 6

Phase Three: Mount Up!

Congratulations! You are well on your way to a solid partnership with your horse. He now has a pretty good idea about his place in the human/horse pecking order and respects you as the "boss" horse. Because you've learned to read the messages he sends via his body language, he trusts that you'll allow him to figure out the next lessons at his own pace. He can rely on you to keep his stress level way under the boiling point. He's begun to be able to shift his weight forward, back, and sideways in response to your cues from the ground. He's worn a saddle and bridle and accepted them as part of his world. You've made a lot of progress with RESISTANCE FREE training. Share the credit with your horse for work well done.

Now, in Phase Three, you'll finally get to sit in the saddle and start his education as a performance horse. This step is like his leaving grammar school for the big league world of high school! But like any freshman, just because he's tall enough for the basketball team doesn't necessarily mean his body is mature enough yet. He's going to need time and miles to build his stamina and fine-tune his athletic responses. So we'll begin slowly with the basics. As I've said before, "Take as much time as it takes" to keep adding to the solid foundation you've been building block by block, RESISTANCE FREE.

EXPAND LONGEING WORK

You are now going to begin to build on the horse's checking experience from Chapter Five and teach him about bending while he's on the longe line. Tack him up and head to the training pen. Work him for a few minutes in each direction at both walk and trot. If he seems stiff in one direction, keep him going a few minutes longer to supple that side. As a general rule, I recommend you work him longer on circles in his stiffer direction—about two to one.

Once he's warmed up in both directions, bring him into the center of the pen and tie the *inside* rein—for example, the left rein, if he'll be working on a circle to the left—to the stirrup to encourage a slight bend in his neck, just as you did when you "checked" him in the stall. He'll respond to the direct pressure of the rein by flexing toward it. When you use a direct rein to create bend, his hindquarters will follow the same path as his forehand in all gaits as he works on the circle. This response in the horse applies to both groundwork and work with a rider. (In the following section on long lining, you'll learn about the use of indirect rein aids.)

Send him back out on the circle and walk and trot him again. Make frequent transitions between gaits to get him used to the idea of flexing and yielding to the direct rein throughout changes in his movement.

Once he accepts this new request to bend toward the inside rein, ask him to go into the lope or canter for a few steps, and then bring him back to the trot. If the transition is smooth, ask him again. Then come back to the trot after a half circle, and ask him to halt. Untie the rein, praise him and rub his favorite spot, and let him stretch his neck down for a minute or two. Then attach the other rein—now the inside rein—to the other stirrup and repeat the above in the opposite direction. If this is his stiff side, for now only ask for a *few* more strides than you did in the easier direction. At this point, just let him adjust to this new idea of flexing his stiff side while going forward. There's plenty of time down the road for more intensive work.

LONG LINING

Now that the horse has been "checked" in both directions on a circle and has become obedient in giving his head to bit pressure, it's time to hook up two longe lines or ropes twelve-to-fifteen-feet long and do some basic long lining where you control the horse from the ground. Some call this work "ground driving," but I refer to this exercise as long lining. I learned my technique from gaited-horse trainers.

Initially, I suggest you attach the lines to the cheek rings of a correctly adjusted halter (fig. 6.1). (A longeing cavesson also works well for this work.) Introduce this lesson with the help of a handler, who can lead the horse through the first lesson or two while you accustom him to the lines touching his sides and to having you behind him. As you'll see in the photographs, I wear protective gloves and recommend you do, as well. Be careful not to loop the line around your wrists or fingers, and hold the extra lengths of line up off the ground so you do not trip on them or become entangled.

Start the horse with a little "cluck" while your assistant leads the horse forward the first couple of times until he understands that you are behind him but still want him to move forward. Move your feet in time with his rhythm, which will help you develop timing for when you get on his back. To stop him, give a light pull on the lines and say, "Whoa." When the horse stops, immediately yield the pressure on the lines. Soon your horse will gain confidence and move forward at your request. At this point, you may feed out the lines so you are walking further behind him and begin to work on turns in both directions (figs. 6.2 to 6.4).

Once you and your horse understand the basics of long lining and he is calm and obedient working off the halter, it's time to make the transition to a bridle. It's also a good opportunity to accustom the horse to wearing tack on his back. You should run the lines through the stirrups of an English saddle tied up as in fig. 6.5. This helps the horse find his balance. If you choose to use a **stock** saddle, you don't need to run the lines through the stirrups. It tends to create an artificially low head and neck position and may confuse the horse in his later training about what is correct. By not going through the stirrups of a Western saddle, you keep the horse a lot lighter and he is less likely to go **behind the bit**.

You can also use a surcingle instead of an English saddle. It has the same effect.

If you find that the horse seems stiff and uncomfortable working in the bit, this is a red light. He won't be able to learn this lesson. As a solution, you might want to use a side pull bridle if he's got a soft nose and gives to pressure. When the side pull is correctly adjusted up by the cheekbones, it is very effective (fig. 6.6).

Now that your horse is outfitted with a bridle and saddle, or surcingle, it's time to head to the round pen. The round pen is an excellent tool at

6.1 to 6.12 Long Lining

6.1 Begin by attaching longe lines or one-inch cotton ropes—12 to 15 feet long—to the check rings of a correctly adjusted halter.

6.2 When you first begin the long-lining process, recruit an assistant to guide the horse until he understands your cues. Note that I'm wearing protective gloves and have the ropes coiled safely in my hand and not dragging along the ground.

6.3 Training sessions in long lines offer good opportunities to begin working in time to your horse's rhythm. Walk in step with him and keep the lines about this length until the work is easy.

6.4 Gradually feed out the lines while maintaining forward motion. At this point, you should be controlling the horse with your long lines and your assistant only should be there in case the horse needs momentary correction.

RESISTANCE FREE *Training*

6.5 On an English saddle secure the stirrups as in this photo and run the lines through them.

6.6 A side pull bridle offers an alternative if your horse has difficulty with the snaffle bit. They are often very effective for sensitive horses.

this stage because the horse will be guided in a circle by the shape of the enclosure. This is especially helpful if you are working on your own. For obvious reasons, never take a green horse out in a large field for this initial lesson.

Your horse should be familiar with having you "drive" him from behind. Now you will accustom him to you standing at his hip as you did when you longed him (fig. 6.7). It would be terribly difficult to work the horse at all gaits if you always had to keep up with him from behind! Long lining from the side is safer, too, plus you can see more of what the horse is doing. When I begin in this position, I like to play out about seven feet of line for early work. Remember to coil the excess line in your hands as you work. When the horse begins to settle into the routine and is happily going forward, you can feed out a little more line at a time until he's about 12 feet out. This results in the horse working on a circle 24 feet in diameter.

Some long-liners start way out on the end of their lines and overuse the lines to cue the horse, causing him to overbend and come behind the bit. They tend to use the strength of their entire bodies, which isn't necessary and just makes the horse heavy. Avoid this scenario. The horse does

6.7 When you are ready to long line solo, use the round pen because its shape offers guidance to your horse and gives you more control.

6.8 Once you feel work is going smoothly in the round pen, move to a larger enclosed area such as a paddock. This additional space will be helpful as you teach the horse to change direction.

6.9 Here the horse is showing me "green lights." He's yielding nicely to the bit and looks relaxed and attentive.

seek a little more contact for security when long lining, but don't haul him around. If you have done your longeing work correctly and have "checked" the horse on both sides, he'll understand and yield to light pressure. Be ready to return to earlier work if he isn't ready for this more demanding lesson.

If your horse is responding well to your cues to walk, trot, and halt in the round pen, you can move into a larger enclosed area such as a ring or a paddock (figs. 6.8 and 6.9). This will offer you plenty of space to begin incorporating changes of direction. At the walk, prepare to turn left by taking up more contact in your left rein, raising your left hand a little bit, and as the horse yields, keeping a little snugness on your right (indirect) rein. The key to smooth turns is to lift the inside rein during the turn. As the turn is completed, bring the new outside rein over the

saddle and across the hindquarters (figs. 6.10 and 6.11). Some horses are initially frightened by the lines passing over their hindquarters. If your horse is clamping his tail and spooking when the lines cross over, keep working with him by gently shifting the lines back and forth until he quietly accepts the situation. If he really panics, don't out-muscle him. Bring him back to a slower walk and rebuild his confidence with work he's shown is already easy for him before practicing the line crossing again. Keep things quiet and easy.

Long lining will also give you a golden opportunity to begin building on the Twelve-Step Program and improve your horse's hip flexibility and movement with some basic lateral work. Use the outside (indirect) rein against his hindquarters as you circle, putting slight pressure on it with the line. You will likely find it easiest

6.10 I'm about to ask my horse to turn to the left so I've taken up more contact with the left line in preparation for my change in direction.

6.11 The horse has turned to the left in answer to my raised left line and I've slid both lines across his hindquarters as we head off in the opposite direction.

6.12 Here again, this gray horse is showing me lots of "green lights." (Note the indirect right rein runs across the seat of the Western stock saddle.)

to do this positioned behind the horse. As soon as the horse begins to give in to this pressure by stepping over, release it. Repeat, and this time bring his hindquarters in slightly, which will require him to step more under his body with his inside hind leg. If the horse is reluctant, use reversals (changes of direction) with the line around his hindquarters instead of over the saddle, changing the pressure points and encouraging him to respond to the pressure of the line. Your first goal is to get the horse to step away from the pressure of the outside (indirect) rein.

For example, let's say you are going to the right. Raise your right hand and bend the horse to the right. Let the left (indirect) line come out and around his left hip, and snug it up slightly to hold him in place. His body will curve, just as

it will eventually do with the aid of your outside leg behind the cinch or girth. As he bends to the right in answer to your right line, tighten the left (indirect) line a little so that he takes one step away from it. This step away from the left line will require him to step more under himself with his right hind leg. This exercise will improve your horse's balance.

After he is solid with long-lining basics—usually two to three sessions—you can go out and tour the neighborhood. You can even go out on little "trail rides." Use obstacles as natural aids to improve his handling ability. This is a good way to introduce him to the world in a safe and secure way.

Here are some **green lights** to watch for as you long line. Your horse should yield easily to

HAND YIELD

The hand yield is one of my favorite training tools for getting a horse on the bit or in the bridle. Stop the horse and ask him to step back by pulling on the left rein. The left shoulder and foreleg should move. Release the left rein and pull on the right rein, asking the right shoulder to yield and move backward. This is a hand yield. The hand yield creates obedience and suppleness as the horse gives and softens in the poll. When the horse gives to the hand, he becomes able to use his shoulders and body to balance himself under a rider.

Your hands must remain soft and flexible, never fixed and "pulling." Rigid hands basically force the horse to break at the third vertebra in the neck, a major fault that places the horse's weight primarily on the forehand and impedes his athletic balance and ability. The rider that develops excellent feel and release of the reins will be best able to refine the horse with the hand yield.

the bit and chew it comfortably and accept rein movement over his topline. He should drop his head and show an overall softness of attitude (fig. 6.12). **Red lights** would include pulling on your hands, taking excessive hold, or lack of overall control. If you are faced with these kinds of problems, do more circles and lateral work if necessary to correct these tendencies. When your horse is long lining well, he should be adept at the walk and jog, and readily reverse direction, stop, and back up. Never underestimate the value of long lining. It really prepares a horse for success later in his career.

However, I don't continue with a lot more long lining other than the basics. I just establish control and softness, then go on with work under saddle. Unless you're going to drive a horse in harness, long lining can become a dead end. You don't want to get so involved it that you fail to progress when the horse needs to move on. Too much long lining tends to make a horse "heavy," just as overuse of side reins and draw reins can. The horse will hang and lean instead of staying light. I have the same criticism of running martingales or any devices that interfere with letting the reins give clean, clear signals. So do enough to get the horse comfortable with this new way of carrying himself until he's obedient to your aids, and then continue his education by getting him accustomed to a rider.

The advantages of long lining are:

1. The horse doesn't have to carry weight while he furthers his training.
2. You can make progress while working in a small area, such as a round pen.
3. It is good preparation for riding.
4. It gets the horse used to something over his back and croup.

It's extremely difficult to train your horse further than you have gone yourself. Remember to add new skills to bring back to your horse.

FIRST MOUNTING

Now that the stage has been set and your young horse is confident in his handler and himself, we'll take his education to the next level: working under a rider. Tack him up, head for the training pen, and keep safety as your top priority. Before you prepare to mount up for the first time, make sure the horse has a good attitude: he should be watching you while standing quietly in the center of the pen. If he can't stand quietly and watch you, that is a red light telling you that he needs more groundwork before you proceed.

If he is quiet, proceed to do **Patterning** work with mounting and dismounting. I personally like to bring an older, quiet "pony horse" into the ring to give the colt extra confidence. Have the rider position his pony horse beside the youngster, to show him this is no big deal. As I've said before, horses learn very well by watching other horses—there is a big difference in the confidence and future progress of a young horse who learns new experiences in the presence of a pony horse. This experience lays an excellent foundation. If you don't have access to a pony horse, work with a ground handler.

The pony rider or ground handler should hold the young horse while you prepare him for his first experience with a rider in the saddle. Put a little weight in the stirrup using your hand, rub the horse when he accepts this sensation, and walk away. If the horse responds to weight in the stirrup by stiffening, or raises his head with tension, resume this step only after he relaxes once more.

The horse should learn to accept you placing your hand anywhere on the saddle or stirrup. Then he should learn that it's okay if you have your left hand in the stirrup and your right hand over the top of the saddle. Next he should get accustomed to the placement of a foot in the stirrup. Be sure that you rest your toe against the cinch, not in the horse's belly. The horse is much more comfortable and less likely to move away from you if you make use of the cinch as a buffer. You see so many careless riders "goosing" the horse in the ribs or elbow as they mount, and often their horses walk off as they mount. That's a pattern you do not want to develop, so keep him comfortable and avoid jabbing him.

Here's how we "Pattern" this experience. Step almost all of the way up, pause momentarily, and step quietly back down. Do this several times. Then step partway up and bounce lightly up and down, to introduce movement combined with weight. Do this several times; increase the weight

and motion if the horse is accepting this experience well. Anytime he flashes a red light, drop the intensity, give him a minute to quiet, and resume when you see those familiar green lights.

When the horse is quiet and ready, step up, but this time, rest your upper body across the saddle. Depending on his reaction, you might need to Pattern this step. If he's nonchalant about it, go ahead and slip up quietly. Shorten the inside rein and lift your leg over his back. When you sit down in the saddle, sit quietly and softly. Don't plop your rear end down as though you were collapsing onto the couch to watch television. Think of the seat of the saddle as a very large egg that you don't want to break. The young horse shouldn't feel the equivalent of a ton of bricks collapsing onto his tender back (figs. 6.13 to 6.17).

Keep your shoulders over your hips as you mount, and you will be able to rise and sit more softly. Letting your shoulders fall behind your **center** puts you off balance and makes mounting more of a struggle. Keep your lower back soft and remember to breath and center yourself. Mount and dismount 25 or 30 times in a session—from alternate sides to train both sides of the horse. This work should be repeated over the course of several days. If the horse is "popping" his tail, raising his head or showing other resistances, these are red lights telling you that he needs more work. Take it slowly and make it easy. This will really pay off.

Rub the horse repeatedly in front of the withers and over the dock of his tail. After you are mounted and have picked up your stirrups, keep your legs quiet. Have the pony rider or handler move the horse around a little bit and let him get used to this new feeling. Keep these first "rides" short and sweet.

Use the Stall

You can also do this mounting work in your box stall, as is done with Thoroughbred racing stock. Be sure you have adequate ceiling height, and

6.13 to 6.17 First Mounting

6.13 Put pressure on the stirrup as you rest your right arm across the saddle.

6.14 Next, place your left hand on his neck and hold the horn with your right as you place your left foot in the stirrup. Bounce up and down lightly, and then with more weight, to get the horse used to movement.

RESISTANCE FREE *Training*

6.15 Now step up and rest your upper body across the saddle.

6.16 Shorten the inside (left) rein as you lift your right leg over his back. Settle softly into the saddle.

6.17 Keep your lower back soft, then exhale and center yourself. Mount and dismount 25 or 30 times each training session until your horse is completely used to the procedure.

use a ground helper who works really well with you.

Both of you should always be on the same side of the horse when working with him. That way, if he does move, he isn't going to run over one of you. If the horse does move, let him go in a circle in the stall. He isn't going anywhere. Go through the exact same sequence as detailed above. Approach, perform a movement, and walk away from the horse. Approach, repeat, and depart. Gradually you ask more and more until you have arrived at the point where the horse is ready to have you mount for the first time.

Remember to keep your toe in the girth, step almost all of the way up, pause momentarily, and step quietly back down. Do it slowly and easily. If the horse raises his head, moves his ears quickly, or holds his breath, step back and rub him a little bit. Walk him around the stall before you resume work. Once you are on board, let the ground person take over moving the horse around inside of the stall. Keep your legs quiet.

If you "Pattern" the horse slowly and quietly, the first mounting will go smoothly and easily. Take your time, build trust in your horse, and you will create a horse who stands quietly for mounting and dismounting on both sides.

MOVING OUTSIDE

Keep in mind that there are complications in training a horse to be ridden because you add your weight to the equation of movement, which changes his balance. He must learn to perform to our standards while carrying the equivalent of a tall, heavy backpack in ways that would never occur to him in a natural situation. Help him figure out his job by taking charge of your own balance.

If you have a "pony horse" establish forward motion with its help. Have the pony rider release your young horse and let you ride around behind his mount. Over the next several days repeat this basic work, following the pony horse until everything is solid.

He should learn to stop and turn on your command with the help of your pony horse or ground person. Let the pony horse help you stop at first. Next, pick up your reins and let that contact tell the horse to stop. Ask him to move his nose left and right, laying the outside indirect rein across his neck as you do so. Remember to keep your hands in a small area—"in the box."

Always ride with two hands when using a snaffle, particularly a broken snaffle bit. Remember that the horse has two sides—work them both! Follow each move from your helper using your legs and reins. When the ground helper or pony rider turns, use the reins to ask the young horse to turn. He will begin to associate the rein cues with the movement. Then he learns that he can do these movements all alone.

Next, do this work without the pony horse in the pen. You have a green light if the young horse stands there quietly and securely, all alone, on a loose rein. You may still want someone to hold his head, but the goal, of course, is ultimately to have him "go it alone." When you ask the horse to move independently for the first time, ask him to shift to the side, not straight ahead. If he does jump when he moves under your weight, relax and go with him, thinking "Jell-O." Any quick movements here give the horse something to resist and fear.

During these initial independent sessions under saddle, you begin to put forward motion on your horse. Move the horse in a circle instead of straight ahead to set yourself up for success and quietness. He can misbehave less if he is bent slightly to turn. Also the act of turning automatically brings the head down slightly and lowering his head will calm him. These factors work together to make this a positive experience.

Goals to achieve in early mounting and dismounting work.

1. Forward motion, stopping, and turning.

2. Staying light, and not violating the horse's space.

Rein Reminders

You can really develop a nice horse if you ride with a feel for balance and a release of the rein. This finesse encourages the horse to try his heart out for you. Use your fingers like sponges. It only takes a few rides with bad hands to set a horse back severely. Just pulling back on both reins at the same time with a yank will cause a horse to stiffen and brace against you.

I have a teaching exercise I like to use between two people. They stand facing one another, one person (the "horse") holds the end of a rein with her eyes closed, and the second person holds the other end of the rein. The idea is to see how far the second person can move the rein before the "horse" feels it move. This exercise teaches people how subtle the "feel" can be. As I always say, if a horse can feel a fly on his hip, he can feel the slack in his rein.

Nice and Easy

Now that you're finally in the saddle, don't be in a hurry to get out of the walk yet. You can easily spend the first ten days just getting the stop and turn down perfectly at the walk. Use your legs in a whisk-broom motion with a bump, bump, bump cue, rather than a harsh, continuous squeeze. The horse tends to back off and lean on continuous pressure, instead of responding lightly as we want to see. Support and develop confidence in your horse. Ask him to walk out in a forward manner. When you stop or turn, use the reins as though you are squeezing out a sponge and encourage the horse to work off of the slack instead of pressure. Use plenty of Preparatory Commands to tune him in to upcoming changes and stay as light as possible. Stay in a small training pen where the horse is quiet and secure.

The lightness in your horse reflects the quality of your groundwork. If you took the time to "check" him in both directions, it's going to pay off when you ride. If he shows resistance when first being ridden this is a red light that tells you that you took a shortcut back in the groundwork.

Don't set him up to brace and tighten against you. Keep your touch sensitive and your body **centered**. Remember that any time you force this horse or jam him around, you're "robbing the future" and stealing from his potential. If you steal too much, you soon won't have any deposits left in the bank to draw from. If you push him too quickly, he won't hold on to his training. You may get a momentary response and some instant control, but you won't have it over the long run.

If you hurry into trot work before this basic framework is solidly laid, you will be more inclined to "snatch" at the horse if something doesn't go well. By putting the first ten days under saddle solely into walk work, you will progress more rapidly down the training sequence in the future because the horse is more trusting. When you've got your basics at the walk, add trotting along the rail to his work. Use lots of transitions to the walk to help him find his balance. Go easy while he builds muscle and endurance. Take it slow: you'll find you get there faster.

THE TWELVE-STEP PROGRAM UNDER SADDLE

Once your horse has a little "forward" to his walk, it's time to revisit the first six steps of the Twelve-Step Program you did on the ground from Chapters Four and Five—this time replacing your hand on his barrel with your calf. When you do these exercises, keep your toes forward in the stirrups, place your calf just behind the cinch, and apply pressure in time with the movement of his feet, just as you did earlier on the ground with your hand. When you cue your horse to move his shoulders, lift your reins to signal forward motion, then cue sideways motion with your calf. This sequence will test and refine your timing.

When you're both in sync, the horse's movement will become fluid and rhythmic. But avoid overdoing it. If the horse gets "cold" from endless repetition, it'll be like riding a hay bale. So keep it simple and build up gradually. Going slowly now will pay off in the years to come.

Make sure he has a basic understanding of "whoa" and "go" at the trot before you introduce Steps 3 and 4. It's fine to do Steps 5 and 6 before you develop his trot.

Step 1: Hips Right at the Walk

◆ Ride toward the fence line at a walk. A couple of steps away, evenly pick up your reins to engage his hindquarters and move your hands slightly to the left.

◆ Cue your horse to move his hips to the right by pressing with your left leg. Press in time with the movement of his hind feet.

◆ Hold his shoulders with the left rein as his hindquarters move in a quarter turn, until he's parallel with the fence.

◆ Ride away at a walk (figs. 6.18 to 6.20).

Step 2: Hips Left at a Walk

◆ Ride toward the fence at a walk. As you approach, pick up the reins to engage his hindquarters. Move your hands to the right.

◆ Use your right leg to cue him to shift his hips to the left.

◆ With the right rein, hold his shoulders as he moves his hindquarters in a quarter turn, until he's parallel to the fence.

◆ Let him settle and then ride off at a walk (figs. 6.21 to 6.24).

Steps 3 and 4:
Hips Right, then Left, at the Trot

◆ Ride to the fence line at a trot.

◆ Repeat Step 1.

◆ Repeat Step 2.

Step 5 and 6:
Forehand Turn, Hips Right, Then Left

◆ Walk to the fence line and stop facing it.

◆ Lift the right rein to maintain the horse's shoulder position.

◆ Press with your left leg to ask the horse to move his hips to the right and pivot on his forehand. Time your leg cues in sync with the movement of his hind feet.

◆ Do a quarter turn on the forehand until he's parallel to the fence.

◆ Hold your left rein steady to maintain his shoulder position.

◆ Press with your right calf to ask the horse to move his hips to the left and pivot on his forehand. Time your leg cues in sync with the movement of his hind feet.

◆ Do a quarter turn, so he's facing the fence (figs. 6.25 to 6.28).

Correction does much,
but encouragement does more.
Encouragement after correction is like
the sun after a rain shower.

6.18 to 6.28 Twelve-Step Program Under Saddle—Steps 1 to 6

6.18 to 6.20 Hips Right at Walk, Step 1

6.18 Step 1a: (Top left) Ride straight toward the fence at a walk. At the fence, pick up your reins to engage the hindquarters and apply pressure with your left leg to move the horse's hips to the right.

6.19 Step 1b: (Top right) Use the left rein to hold the shoulders until the horse is parallel to the fence.

6.20 Step 1c: (Left) Ride away at a walk.

6.21 to 6.24 Hips Left at Walk, Step 2

6.21 Step 2a: At a walk, ride directly to the fence, then pick up the reins to engage his hindquarters.

6.22 Step 2b: Use your right leg to cue him to shift his hips to the left.

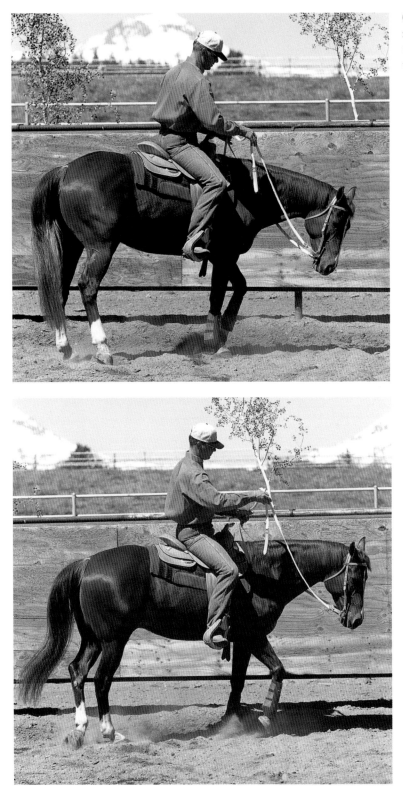

6.23 Step 2c: Hold his shoulders with the reins until the horse is parallel to the fence.

6.24 Step 2d: Let your horse settle, and then ride off at a walk.

Hips Right, then Left at Trot—Steps 3 and 4 are ridden similarly to Steps 1 and 2.

6.25 to 6.27
Forehand Turn, Hips
Right, Step 5

6.25 Step 5a: Begin
facing the fence. Lift
the right rein to hold
the shoulder. Apply
pressure with the left
leg to shift the hip to
the right and pivot on
his forehand.

6.26 Step 5b: Coordi-
nate your leg-pressure
cues: press every time
he lifts his left hind
foot.

6.27 Step 5c: As he shifts his hips, he pivots on his front end in this turn on the forehand. End the movement parallel to the fence. Step 6 begins from here. Reverse all cues, ending up facing the fence as you were when you began Step 5.

6.28 Forehand Turn, Hips Left, Step 6: After completing a forehand turn, hips right with your horse parallel to the fence, reverse all the cues in Step 5. This horse has almost finished his turn, hips left, and will end up directly facing the fence.

Lesson Plan: Phase Three

The Clock Drill, the Independent Engagement Drill, and backing exercises continue daily, as well as basic work on the longe line. Fine-tune your work in the Twelve-Step Program On the Ground exercises a little each day.

Step 1

The horse is checked to the inside stirrup, just short enough to encourage a slight bend, and worked on the longe line at the walk and trot in both directions. When the horse is moving smoothly, begin to add work at the lope. Ponying also continues.

Step 2

Long lining begins. Focus on going forward and turning at the walk.

Step 3

A steady "pony horse" is brought in and Patterning work in preparation for mounting begins. Mount and dismount the young horse 25 to 30 times, working from both sides. Then ride the young horse around the round pen in a good forward walk while following the companion horse, and end the lesson for the day.

Step 4

Using the training reins as side reins, check the horse up to both stirrups, and longe him. Watch for him to begin to balance himself, particularly at the lope. Then build further on the saddle work from the previous day. Ride the young horse in the round pen behind the older horse and ask him to do some stops and turns. Introduce trotting along the rail for the first time. Begin to watch for some good moves from this young horse as he learns to balance a rider.

Step 5

To transfer lessons on the ground to his education under saddle, introduce the horse to Steps 1 to 6 of the Twelve-Step Program to refine his responsiveness and suppleness.

Step 6

This basic work continues through the remainder of Phase Three. Confirm that the horse is accepting his new role as a saddle-horse-in-training and keep your requests simple and soft. Use Preparatory Commands before you ask for a change in direction or speed. Slowly build up your time in the saddle, making sure you help him maintain his balance and calm by staying balanced and calm yourself.

Give him the seventh day off to rest and to process these important changes in his life.

CHAPTER 7

Phase Four: Continue Building Obedience

The exercises in Phase Four take your horse's basic education to the next level. Now we'll be working toward refining his movement and responses. By the end, you'll have built a solid foundation for whatever future training goals you have.

Begin these more advanced lessons only after your horse is giving you green lights in the earlier work. I can't tell you how long that might take, but your horse will. By now you know how reliable his messages are about how ready he is to take his schooling one step further.

COMPLETE THE TWELVE-STEP PROGRAM UNDER SADDLE

These final steps of the Twelve-Step Program Under Saddle will improve lead changes, enhance collection and straightness, and refine your work on circles.

Steps 7: Haunches Turn, Shoulders Right

◆ Face away from the fence.

◆ With even hands, lift the reins and shift them slightly to the right to move the shoulders. At the same time...

◆ Press with your left leg to ask the horse to move his shoulders to the right, as he pivots on his hindquarters. Cue with leg and rein when he steps down and again when his feet lift. Hold his hindquarters stationary with your right leg.

◆ Do a quarter turn until he's parallel with the fence (figs.7.1 to 7.4).

Steps 8: Haunches Turn, Shoulders Left

◆ With even hands, lift the reins and shift them slightly to the left to move the shoulders. At the same time...

◆ Press with your right calf to ask the horse to move his shoulders to the left, as he pivots on his hindquarters. Cue with leg and rein when he steps down and again when his feet lift. Hold his hindquarters stationary with your left leg.

◆ Do a quarter turn until he's parallel to the fence (figs. 7.5 to 7.8.)

7.1 to 7.11 Twelve-Step Program Under Saddle—Steps 7 to 12

7.1 to 7.4 Haunches Turn, Shoulders Right, Step 7

7.1 Step 7a: (Facing page, upper left) Stand with the fence at your back and pick up both reins to take the shoulders to the right.

7.2 Step 7b: (Facing page, upper right) Use your left leg to cue him to move his shoulders as he pivots with his hindquarters.

7.3 Step 7c: (Facing page, bottom) In this haunches turn to the right, his right hind foot remains stationary.

7.4 Step 7d: (Top) Apply leg and rein pressure as the horse steps down and again when he lifts his feet, until he's parallel to the fence.

7.5 to 7.8 Haunches Turn, Shoulders Left, Step 8

7.5 Step 8a: (Top left) Face away from the fence. Pick up both reins to move the shoulders to the left.

7.6 Step 8b: (Top right) In the haunches turn to the left, his hindquarters pivot as his shoulders move left.

7.7 Step 8c: (Right) Watch for level ears and that the right front leg crosses in front of the left leg. The left hind is the stationary pivot foot. The rider's left leg holds the hindquarters stationary.

7.8 Step 8d: Finish parallel to the fence.

Step 9: Hip Out

◆ Ride at a walk parallel to the fence, which is on your left.

◆ Keep the reins steady to maintain the horse's shoulder position.

◆ Press with your right calf to cue him to move his hips to the left, toward the fence.

◆ Continue along the fence for four or five strides, keeping his shoulders parallel to the fence as his hindquarters travel on a track to the outside of the shoulders (fig. 7.9).

◆ Release the pressure from your right leg and left rein and allow the horse to straighten and come onto one track for several strides.

◆ Repeat a maximum of four times.

7.9 Hip Out, Step 9: Walk parallel to the fence. Hold the horse's shoulders steady with even reins. Apply pressure with the right leg in rhythm with the hind steps to shift the hips toward the fence, while his shoulders remain parallel to fence. Then allow the horse to straighten.

Step 10: Hip In

- Ride at a walk parallel to the fence, which is on your left.
- Keep the left rein steady to maintain the horse's shoulder position parallel to the fence.
- Press with your left leg to cue him to move his hips to the right, away from the fence.
- Continue along the fence for four or five strides, keeping his shoulders in place as his hindquarters travel on a track to the inside of the shoulders (fig. 7.10).
- Release the pressure from your left leg and right rein and allow the horse to straighten and come onto one track for several strides.
- Repeat a maximum of four times.

Step 11: Sidepass Right

- Walk your horse forward.
- With your hands even, lift the reins and shift them to the right to cue the horse to move his shoulders to the right. At the same time...
- Cue him to move his haunches to the right with your left calf.
- Then alternate pressure: shift the reins when the horse steps with his front feet; press with your left leg when he steps with his hind feet.
- Sidepass four or five steps, working toward straightness, balance, and fluid motion in horse and rider (fig. 7.11).

Step 12: Sidepass Left

- Walk your horse forward.
- With your hands even, lift the reins and shift them to the left to cue the horse to move his shoulders to the left. At the same time...
- Cue him to move his hips to the left with your right calf.

7.10 Hip In, Step 10: Walk along parallel to the fence. While you use even pressure on both reins to hold the horse's shoulders steady, apply pressure with your left leg in time with the hind steps to shift the hips away from the fence for four or five strides. Then allow the horse to straighten.

- Then alternate pressure: shift the reins when the horse steps with his front feet; press with your right leg when he steps with his hind feet.
- Sidepass four or five steps, working toward straightness, balance, and fluid motion in horse and rider.

7.11 Sidepass to the Right, Step 11: To sidepass to the right, move the shoulders right by lifting the reins. At the same time, cue with the left leg to shift the haunches right. Time your rein cues to his front steps, and your leg cues to his hind steps, to keep him straight and balanced. For Step 12, reverse your cues for the Sidepass to the Left.

HARMONIOUS CIRCLES

Circles promote rhythm and cadence. Done correctly, they also promote straightness, which means the horse's hind feet will follow the same track as his front feet, whether on straight lines or around curves. Circles give you hip, shoulder, and rib-cage control. This is a natural progression from the longeing and training-pen work that encourages the horse to engage behind. The horse's mental attitude is softer and more in tune with the rider than when working on the straight in the ring, or on a trail ride. As his fitness increases, use circles often. Once he's mentally and physically fit, you can never do too many circles.

Circles bring harmony and unity to horse and rider. All the trainers I've worked with, particularly in the reining, working-cowhorse, and cutting disciplines, use circles 75 percent of their training time.

As the rider, it's your job to offer the horse consistent balance and support through your hands and legs. Your horse relies on that for security. In any circle, you use your inside leg in support of the inside rein and hand to keep the inside shoulder up (not falling in) and arc the body properly. A loose rein is not appropriate in the training stage. Your reliable contact allows your horse to relax into steady rhythms on the circle.

The outside leg keeps the hip in and holds the ribcage there. The outside leg is further back, just behind the girth; your inside leg is at the girth. The legs are used in a whisk-broom motion, not as clamps.

Focus on keeping your circles round like an orange, not lop-sided like an egg. The rider can really promote a good circle by always keeping his hands steady and quiet. Take up the contact just the slightest little bit on the inside rein and lift the inside hand a little to keep the shoulder up.

The young horse will tell you the size of the circle he can do. Find the arc that keeps him forward and relaxed. Work there until his green lights tell you he's got it figured out, then ask him to find his balance on larger and smaller arcs. When you can expand, then shrink, and expand your circle again, you've made significant progress. Naturally, this isn't going to

PROBLEM-SOLVING: LEADS

When a horse finds picking up the correct lead difficult, I place a pole on the ground so that he has to reach up and make a little jump over it. As he approaches in the jog and starts to lift over the pole, his shoulder automatically comes up. He gets under himself a little more and begins to use his back more correctly. In order for a horse to lope or canter properly, impulsion has to come from the hindquarters. Even though it seems as though the lope or canter comes from the front when you school over a pole, it's actually coming from behind. The horse lifts his shoulders after he engages his hocks.

The next step is to ask the horse to pick up the lope in the corner of the ring, which has a similar effect to the pole in making him engage and lift. Pick up the horse's inside shoulder with your inside rein, put your weight in the outside stirrup, cluck, and drive with the outside leg.

If you are going down the rail to the left, to make a strike off to the left lead, you pick up the left rein, put your weight in the outside stirrup just slightly, lift the horse's left shoulder and apply the outside leg. Let the horse take himself into the lope.

Going to the right, you pick up the right rein a little, lift the right shoulder, put your weight in the left stirrup very slightly to the outside of the arc, and apply the left leg. Squeeze the outside (left) leg as he pushes off, and release the outside leg when the inside right leg of the horse hits the ground. Coordinate your movements of hand and leg to create a smooth lope strike-off.

With a problem horse, don't hesitate to return to the pole on the ground if he backslides. Do lots of transitions into the lope and teach the horse to trust your hand. Don't let him run off through the bit. Make him set up and control his speed and patience. Make a lope transition as graceful and smooth as water pouring over a waterfall!

A nervous horse will really come unglued if you are chasing him off his feet, kicking and driving him furiously. This pattern of movement will imprint on him permanently if you aren't careful, and his strike-offs will always be poor. Instead, lead your partner in a graceful dance.

happen in your first ride. Keep it in mind as a goal for your work in the days and weeks ahead. Do twice as many circles on the stiff side of your horse as the easy side until he gets more balanced.

When the young horse starts falling on his inside shoulder, or starts cutting the circle, drive him off in a straight line for a few steps and start over, instead of trying to patch up a damaged circle. Get him straight and back under control, then try it again. Until the horse is confirmed between your hands and legs, starting over is the best option.

After you introduce the idea of working on contact on a circle to your young horse in a pen, move on to doing circles in the open or at least off the rail. The horse learns to perform without the aid of a fence to balance against. Begin with a strong, solid walk, then move to the trot. If you are balanced and relaxed in the sitting trot, this position is more secure and gives the horse more confidence than a posting trot. Be sure that he can do good quality circles at a walk and trot before you move on to the lope.

Ultimately the horse develops confidence and trust in his rider. Your hands and legs will set the arc and the rhythm. Reward the horse generously when he responds to this new challenge with honest effort.

Obedience is built one step at a time.

PREPARE FOR THE SHOULDER-MOVE DRILL

As I said early in Chapter Five when we began to work with the concept of "inside" and "outside," generally the horse is bent to the inside when working on circles, especially in his early training: his hindquarters stay on the path traveled by his forehand. Now that the horse is further in his training, we'll look the idea of counter-bending, which is when the horse is bent away from his direction of movement. Often his front and hind ends will follow different tracks. This lateral flexion creates an athletic horse by increasing his strength, balance, and flexibility. For instance, the Shoulder-Move Drill that follows uses counter-bending to supple the horse's shoulders. To see an example of how counter-bending works in action, let's look at the counter-canter.

As you'll learn in the following section on leads, normally when you ask for a canter (or lope) depart going to the right on a circle, the correct leading leg is the foreleg to the inside of the circle—in this case, the right fore. The horse is slightly bent to the inside as he curves in the direction of movement on the circle. However, in a counter-canter to the right, the correct leading leg is the left foreleg, nearest the rail. The horse will now be slightly bent to the left as he canters on the circle in a counterclockwise (right) direction. His left side becomes his inside. In this case, the inside of the arena doesn't correspond to the inside of the horse. And that's because the inside of the bend remains the "inside" of the horse, even when he is bent toward the outside of the arena.

Remember, the inside of the horse corresponds to the inside of his bend. Keep this point in mind when you distinguish between your inside and outside leg and rein aids in this drill.

The Shoulder-Move Drill

Now that you've worked on developing the horse's balance on the circle, here's one more drill to add to your training routine. The Shoulder-Move Drill is a really good exercise for suppling the horse's shoulders. You'll also learn to refine the timing of your inside and outside aids as you negotiate the cones.

This one is fun! Don't be alarmed if a few cones topple over in the process of getting this drill down.

1. Be sure your horse is warmed up and attentive to your aids. Then set up a line of four cones about 12 feet apart and mount up. *(Hint: Especially at first, the cones can be set up further apart if you like. Later, set them 12 feet to emphasize the horse's bend through his shoulders.)*

2. The point of this drill is to slightly bend your horse's head and body in the direction opposite his movement as he passes between the cones. Approach the first cone on a line that's about six feet to the left of the cone. The cone is on your right. Bend his head slightly to the left with a direct left rein and your left leg at the cinch as the horse travels right toward the cone. Support this bend with an indirect right rein and your right leg a little behind the cinch. Activate the

7.12 to 7.16 The Shoulder-Move Drill

7.12 For the Shoulder-Move Drill, set up four traffic cones in a straight line 12 feet apart. To supple the shoulders, use the left rein to counterbend the horse slightly away from the turn as you proceed through the first two cones.

7.13 Time your hands to the rise and fall of the horse's feet for RESISTANCE FREE movement through the cones.

leading right shoulder by pressing with your left leg at the cinch as he steps sideways between the cones. Your goal is for him to step smoothly through the right shoulder and maintain his slight bend away from the direction of travel as he passes in front of the first cone.

3. After you pass the cone going right, prepare to change the horse's bend to the right with both rein and leg aids to allow

him to change his direction of travel to the left back toward the cones. Your leg and rein aids will reverse to encourage and support the new bend away from the new direction of travel. The goal is to meet the challenge of passing between the first and second cones while the horse is bent as smoothly as possible to the new inside.

7.14 (Top left) Change the bend smoothly as you proceed so the horse is stepping through his left shoulder.

7.15 (Top right) The horse is about to turn to the right
again and will counterbend to the left as he did in
photo 7.12.

7.16 (Bottom right) Concentrate on keeping his ears
level with soft leg and rein pressure. When you've
mastered the walk, try this exercise at the trot as in
this series of photos.

4. To prepare for passing between the next
   cones, repeat this shift between leg and
   rein aids again. And so on.
5. When you can pass through four cones
   using soft aids while keeping the horse's
   ears level, try this drill at the trot to really free up his shoulders and refine the
   timing of your aids (figs. 7.12 to 7.16).

CASE STUDY: DOC'S CRACKLE

Doc's Crackle is a three-year-old Quarter Horse gelding who is a quick study. He learned to lead in one day. The same with longeing and long lining. It took only 30 minutes to saddle and put a rider on him the first time, and he mastered the groundwork of the Twelve-Step Program in about a week.

He's been ridden about 30 days and now takes both leads reliably. Should we go ahead and begin schooling him for lead changes, stops, and turns?

Don't be fooled. A lot of really well-bred horses respond quickly to the positive approach of RESISTANCE FREE *training. Their eager response and apparently bottomless capacity for learning can give the impression they can learn it all in the first month. But they still need lots of foundation and time. Young horses are building mind and muscle while they learn. Horses like Doc's Crackle are very athletic, but he's not mentally ready at this stage for advanced movements. Overloading a young horse during this important initial training period may be tempting. He's learned everything you've given him in record time, after all, and seems hungry for more. Resist this impulse in favor of the long-term goal of a sound horse that loves his work for many years to come.*

The transition from building a forward walk-trot-lope and learning to carry and trust the rider to the advanced step of changing leads is a key step in his development. You'll find that the mental pressure to understand and perform flying changes is going to be too much to handle at this point in his development.

Stay with the walk-trot-lope circles and the Twelve-Step Program Under Saddle for at least 120 rides. After he's got that base, you might spend about six minutes during a 45-minute session schooling the changes. Always remember that there are two sides to RESISTANCE FREE *training: the physical and the mental. Let him mature in both mind and body.*

When you boil milk on the stove, you can easily scorch it if you turn up the heat too fast.

LEADS

You've supplied the horse's shoulders with counter-bending through a line of cones. Now, let's take those free shoulders on to a circle at the lope. Because circles and horses both have an inside and an outside, matching them up— that is, making sure that the horse leads with his *left* (inside) fore on a circle to the *left*—is a key point to add to his education.

Leads are important building blocks in the foundation of any horse. A well-schooled horse must be ambidextrous, able to take right or left lead at will and on command. His transitions must be fluid and soft, making it easy to change from movement to movement. Good cutting horses switch leads in a hoofbeat according to how the cow moves. In barrel racing, good lead changes make the difference between picking up a check and going home with nothing but memories. Hunters and jumpers need smooth lead changes to get them set up for the next fence safely and in good time. Whatever your sport, reliable leads are important.

Initial groundwork develops the foundation that leads to ambidexterity and maximizes athletic ability. It also demonstrates to you which side the horse is strong on and which is his awkward side. This gives you the opportunity to concentrate on improving the weak side through exercises such as "checking" and longeing more often in the direction he finds challenging. The goal is to get him to the point where he makes little or no distinction between his good side and his bad side. By now, you should be well on your way to achieving this goal.

The key to getting correct leads on a young horse is to put him in a position that makes it almost impossible for him to make a mistake picking up his leads. I recommend that you choose the direction he finds the easiest for the first experience with leads and lead changes, to tip the scales in his favor.

1. In your larger training area, to set him up to take the left lead, circle the horse left at a balanced, forward trot.

2. Ride him toward the fence (or another barrier), pull his nose left while looking leftward yourself.

3. Lift your left hand just enough to lift his left shoulder up. Keep slack out of the reins.

4. Put your weight in the right (outside) stirrup and drive with your outside leg until he picks up the canter rhythm leading with his left front leg.

Placing weight in the outside stirrup correctly balances you for the first beat of the lope, which makes it easier for the horse to support your weight and feel what is correct. If you lean to the inside, you weigh down the very shoulder that needs freedom of movement in order to pick up the lead. Also, the horse loses the security of your balanced weight on the first beat of the lope. In response, the horse may pick up the wrong lead because that's what you have physically set him up to do.

To repeat, always pull the horse's nose just a little bit in the direction of travel to set him up and then raise the inside hand slightly to lift the inner shoulder. Keep your weight to the outside for support and balance and to free up the inside shoulder. Don't use a slack rein as you introduce him to leads. Instead, take up on the rein just a little to increase his balance and security.

The rider's leg rhythm is important. Just squeezing his barrel like a tube of toothpaste is not productive. The young horse has a tendency to fall into pressure, and if he does that, he'll lean against your leg. It may disturb his balance enough to send him on to the wrong lead. In the lope, your outside leg should go bump, bump, bump, in rhythm. As he pushes off in the first beat of the gait on the outside hind leg, your outside leg should squeeze as he goes into the second beat. Into the third beat, the rider's leg releases. You develop a push-release, push-release sequence, or a gather-and-lope. Good leg rhythm combined with feel and contact will set up a young horse for correct leads.

Don't ask the horse to "gallop" indefinitely while you struggle to get the leads. Avoid chasing him from a jog into an irregular fast trot into a sloppy lope. "Chasing" the horse from gait to gait shows lack of skill and basic understanding of the horse's balance and movement. As a trainer, you need to improve your skills and riding finesse if you want your horse to develop these qualities himself. Move with discipline from a controlled, forward trot at an appropriate tempo to a controlled lope or canter in a true three-beat rhythm.

Good horsemanship is the power to invoke the right response in your horse at the correct time.

DOUBLING

Doubling is a common exercise for young horses in Western horsemanship. In this exercise, the horse will reverse direction by shifting his weight back on his hindquarters as he "rolls over his hocks" toward the new direction of travel. To accomplish this reversal, the horse lifts his shoulders while the hindquarters support his weight through the change in direction. He pivots on the hind leg in the direction of the turn. As he shortens his frame for the reversal, his center of gravity shifts to the rear. A fence or other barrier is often used to help the horse move his **center of gravity** back. This exercise helps teach the Western horse collection much the way lengthening and compressing strides is used in dressage to adjust the horse's center of gravity toward the hindquarters. A bonus of this exercise is the release of tension in the horse's back as he shortens his frame and rounds his back to change his center of gravity.

Doubling teaches the horse to work off of his hindquarters, giving the rider almost instant control of the direction of movement. This exercise benefits the horse that tends to be awkward. It helps pull everything together, like a dribbling exercise for a basketball player. It helps him get his balance and is an important technique for getting control of his shoulders. It also creates deepness in his hocks and strengthens him for advanced work off his hocks later in his career. This move requires some sophisticated riding from you. Balance and timing make all the difference here. When you're ready to test your horsemanship and improve your horse, give it a try.

Start this work in the training pen, either round or square. I recommend teaching this in a snaffle and prefer a full-cheek style, which keeps the bit stable. I've found it's best to work on this move when the horse is fresh, because you're channeling his energy and forward motion. It takes energy and heart to double efficiently. If you wait until he's already tired from a workout, it'll be like dribbling a flat basketball: lots of effort, frustrating results.

1. Trot the horse parallel to the rail, in a counter-clockwise direction to the left, about five feet out from the fence.

2. When you're ready to begin, use the right rein in time with the right hind leg to draw the horse's face toward the fence. Use the left rein for support.

3. As he starts to shift his shoulders to make a turn toward the fence (and not before), put a little weight in the left stirrup: think of this as changing his center of gravity.

7.17 to 7.23 Doubling

7.17 to 7.19 Doubling at a Fence

7.17 (Facing page) Doubling at a fence to the right: once your horse is proficient doing this at the walk, trot or lope parallel to the fence. Turn him toward the fence with your right rein when his right hind is on the ground.

7.18 (Top) You'll feel the horse lower his right hock as he shifts his weight to the rear.

7.19 (Bottom) Once his shoulders shift to the right, apply pressure with your left leg on his barrel to support the turn. Your horse pivots around his right hind leg.

4. You'll feel him set the right hock down beneath your seat as he begins to roll his shoulders to the right. The right leg is the pivot leg for this reverse to the right. Release his head and bump him with the left leg. This frees up the shoulder and front end and causes him to roll over his right hock to the right.

5. Once he's rolled over in a 180-degree turn and is parallel to the fence going right, trot off. You should find his forward motion is improved with this exercise (figs. 7.17 to 7.19).

6. Do something else for a few minutes and then try this exercise in the other direction. Later, when you are both proficient at doubling, try it at the lope.

If the horse is inattentive, use a direct inside rein in a strong, secure pull, followed up by the indirect outside rein, put weight in the outside stirrup, and bring him in toward the fence or barrier until he starts to come over his inside hip. As he commits himself to the turn, give him a lot of release in his face, and you'll feel him lift his back and get his inside pivot foot beneath him.

One of the key points in doubling is not to over-pull. Doubling is a subtle exercise that tests your timing. Done right, doubling teaches the horse balance and correctness.

In a square pen, it's natural to double when coming straight on to your fence. As he shifts his weight back in preparation for the reversal, the corner supports him. On horses with a tendency to be uncoordinated and hollow-backed, use the outside leg with a little more pop. Hurry the horse up and trot him right out of that turn toward the fence. To avoid a collision, he'll really start planting his feet underneath.

If the horse is starting to turn on his forehand or do a "bellybutton turn," turning around his middle so to speak, nine times out of ten you are using too much direct inside rein pull. That's a red-light situation. Go back to just flexing his nose in the new direction, and

when he moves his shoulder, follow up with the indirect outside rein. Less pull will get the job done better.

If the horse shows red lights by turning just his head while his motion goes through the shoulder instead of shifting to the new direction, remember to take up on the indirect outside rein to control the outside shoulder as you double the horse in the new direction.

If the horse jams up and doesn't reverse direction, more than likely this is caused when you use your leg before first getting the shoulders to shift over. This is one of the few exercises when your leg is secondary. The shoulders and the front end have got to move over first, in response to the rein aids. Then you apply the leg after the horse is committed to the change in direction. If you use the leg first, the horse will use the motion to go forward into your hand and gum up the works.

Once you've got this exercise working for you, it's fun to trot around in the open, to double the horse off natural barriers. Out on the trail, use a fence, or a bush. I rode with Californian, Clyde Kennedy, who rode on a rimrock up behind his place. There was a 300-foot drop-off. He often doubled his horses as he trotted along this rimrock. If the horse had run through the bridle or failed to stay over his hocks, it would have been a long drop! I wasn't quite that brave, but I'll often use a tree to set a horse up and make him listen.

Here's a step-by-step for doubling to the left in the open:

1. At a lope, feel for when the left hind drives beneath the horse.

2. Then use your left rein to bring his face to the left. He'll begin to pivot on the left hind.

3. Use your right leg to control and direct the ribcage as he rolls his shoulders to the left.

4. Take a fairly firm hold on the left rein to channel the horse's impulsion into a

7.20 Doubling in the open to the left: this horse is performing at the lope. He has slowed down and as the rider shifts the horse's head to the left, he can feel the left hind support the horse's weight underneath him.

7.21 As he doubles around, use your left leg at the cinch as if it were a pole. Take a fairly firm hold of the left rein to channel his impulsion in a 180-degree turn.

180-degree turn. As your horse doubles around, think of your left leg (keep it at the cinch) as a pole he's circling.

5. Drive out of the change in direction with both legs, keeping your upper body slightly forward to stay with his movement (figs. 7.20 to 7.23).

Doubling in the Open (cont.)

7.22 Support the right shoulder with the right rein.

7.23 Use both legs to drive out of the 180-degree turn at the lope.

Lesson Plan: Phase Four

Continue ground drills and your work on the longe line to reinforce your leadership and increase his mental and physical abilities. Constantly watch for red and green lights during work in the round pen. This young horse should be giving you green lights after only five minutes of longe work. "Check" the young horse slightly more snugly in each direction in this phase.

   Throughout this phase, dismount in different places in the ring. The young horse must never associate one place with dismounting. Instead, the smart trainer dismounts in a different place each day, and if possible, exits the ring from a different gate. This prevents the young horse from anticipating and quitting in front of one "favorite" gate. Add the Shoulder-Move Drill to his list of accomplishments, finish the Twelve-Step Program Under Saddle, build a history of success with leads, and then polish your skills with some smooth "doubles." Always quit on a good note with a quiet, relaxed horse. Then give him a rub on his favorite spot and pat yourself on the back! *(continued on next page)*

Here's a typical lesson plan that we use:

Step 1

Work on the last six steps of the Twelve-Step Program Under Saddle to refine the work you began in Chapters Four, Five, and Six. Work on establishing forward motion through circles and use lots of leg to establish the trot. Use frequent Preparatory Commands and emphasize the slack rein. Have an older horse continue to join you in the pen so that the young one can follow him.

Step 2

If things go well, leave the round pen and ride in the big arena for a few minutes each day. Follow the older horse into the open ring and ride on the rail and across the diagonal, emphasizing good forward motion. Ask for a decent stop, with lots of Preparatory Commands. Look for him to begin to shift his weight off his forehand and on to his hindquarters as he stops.

Step 3

Next, the lope is introduced in the large arena by following another horse on the rail at walk and jog. In preparation for the lope, make a big circle toward the inside of the ring. Upon reaching the rail, ask for the lope. Emphasize that the young horse accepts forward motion generated by the rider's outside leg when moving into the lope. Once you've got the lope established, retire the "pony horse" and start riding the young horse alone.

Step 4

Add the Shoulder-Move Drill to his routine and spend time everyday working lateral-stepping movements of the Twelve-Step Program Under Saddle. Look for level ears and smooth movement, and work toward getting quieter and quieter with your cues.

Step 5

Begin making transitions from gait to gait in the training pen, alternating lope, jog, lope, jog, etc. Emphasize Preparatory Commands. Do lots of circles and "double" off the rail in the pen. It's time to begin work on leads in the square pen, using the corners as an aid.

Step 6

Your horse graduates the Four Phases when he can lope on the correct lead in each direction on the rail and in circles in the big arena. Now you can start using your body weight to shorten and lengthen the lope. If things go well, bring back your "pony horse" and end the day with a short trail ride.

Remember to give him every seventh day to himself to be a horse.

You will notice that we have done no event-specific training at this point. You may have a plan or two in mind, but don't push him too fast. A horse with these basics in place can move forward later in his specific sport, training relatively quickly because he trusts you completely. Sandbagging him with a tough workout at this point would destroy that security.

Train this horse for a long-term career. We'd like to see him last twenty years, not two. Plan his training schedules with that in mind and be aware of the horse's physical state at all times. If he begins to show soreness, back off and take more time. A sore horse isn't going to learn. Let him recover, and cut his schedule down accordingly.

PART 3

Handling Challenges—RESISTANCE FREE

The RESISTANCE FREE training techniques outlined in Chapters One through Seven are very effective for dealing with challenging horses. And chances are, if you work around horses long enough, someday you'll meet up with such a horse. Perhaps you own one now. With the positive focus of RESISTANCE FREE training, I firmly believe that just about any horse can be improved. In Part Three, I'll talk about specific approaches to reeducating horses that have been mishandled, poorly raised, spoiled, or that tend to panic. What every difficult horse needs is a compassionate trainer with high levels of patience and horse sense. A trainer who adds RESISTANCE FREE training techniques to that winning combination really increases his chances for success with the horse that arrives at the barn with a less-than-perfect nature, or history.

CHAPTER 8

Working with Difficult Horses

There are many types of challenging horses that a RESISTANCE FREE trainer may meet up with during his or her career. Maybe you've got one in your barn or stable right now. The training methods outlined in Chapters One to Seven can be the key to "solving" many, if not most, difficult horses. The basic training tools of building trust, interpreting the horse's messages, establishing yourself at the head of the pecking order, and liberal applications of positive reinforcement can help you make lemonade out of horses that right now just look like sour, four-legged lemons.

We'll take a look at four of the more common challenges. These include mishandled or abused horses; horses raised by bad-minded dams that influenced them poorly; horses with an unusually sensitive spirit that are on the verge of panic; and the spoiled pet who lacks respect for the pecking order. Each of these types of horses requires a different approach in training. The trainer must work with these horses to make them mentally ready before normal training can

take place. It's extremely important to their successful reeducation that the people handling these horses have well-developed horse sense, compassion, and the patience to take satisfaction in the smallest improvements.

Here's how RESISTANCE FREE training can change even challenging red lights to green.

MISHANDLED HORSES

Horses that have been mishandled by a trainer or by their owners are regrettably common. They need reassurance in the essential goodness of people before they will open their spirit once more. The abuse may have taken the form of beating, jerking without provocation, or other scenarios intended to bully the horse into submission.

The horses who suffer most are usually involved with people who have unstable personalities and hair-trigger tempers. You've seen those people—quiet one moment and screaming the next. When something doesn't go their way, they blow up all out of proportion about the misplaced pitchfork, the flat tire on the truck, or

CASE STUDY: DOC'S SPECIAL FLOWER

Doc's Special Flower is a small brown mare who has been severely abused. Because she was bred to be a cutting horse, she is extra sensitive and never misses a thing.

Her first owner did not try to halter-break or even touch her until she was seven months old. To introduce her to that important lesson, the owner starved her for two days and then lured her into a pen with some feed. When she entered the pen to go to the food, he and his helpers shut the gate and roped her. She tried to escape and fought until she threw herself down. In the hour it took to halter her and teach her to lead, she lost a tooth and dislocated her neck.

She was not handled again until she was about two years old. Again, in order to lure her into a small pen, she was left without food and water for two days and again roped and haltered when she entered the pen to get to the food. Hobbles were put on her and then she was saddled and mounted for the first time, in about an hour. Each time she tried to escape, the hobbles took her down to the ground.

Next, blankets and ropes were thrown at her in the name of desensitization, but of course what happened was she was traumatized. This time, she suffered rope burns on her legs and neck.

For the next three weeks, she was tied to a snubbing post and fed only hay. Her owner didn't want her too spunky. Next, she was taken to a sale and sold.

The new owner took her home and turned her out. When she wouldn't allow herself to be caught, they chased her down with another horse until she went through a fence and cut herself. The new owner was furious. When he finally caught her, he beat her with a rope.

She was taken out for rides on the trail. The owner got upset when she looked over at a cow, a dog, or a bird. He'd pull her around in a hard circle, yanking on the bit and spurring her sides until she froze and just stopped moving.

Back to the sales she went. Her third owner recognized her breeding and bought her as a cutting horse. Finally she was going to be doing the work she was bred for. However, even though she would instinctively start to work a cow, when the pressure increased and she needed to go to the next level, she would stop and freeze instead. Her history had created a huge roadblock for this horse.

The trainer lost his temper and used his spurs and reins to punish her and try to get her to move on. What he got was a horse with bloody sides and a sore mouth.

At six years old, Doc's Special Flower had been turned into a mare who blew up, ran off, and refused to be caught. Because she was so mishandled in all her early contact with humans, her talent was wasted. It would be like tying Michael Jordan's feet with ropes and forcing him to play basketball. The thing that makes this case even worse is that the victim of the abuse was lured into situations and her trust completely broken by the hurt that followed. Consequently, this mare was about to lose her mind. Nothing to do with people was reliable except rough handling.

How can the current owner ever put trust and confidence back into this horse?

Well, trust and confidence were never there in the first place, so the only place to go is back to the start. This mare needs lots of slow, easy groundwork. Understand that she is going to blow up under the slightest pressure in the beginning, so when she does, back off and go back to square one. Before you end a training session, make sure you can end on a good note. Look for a couple of green lights and make much of her. Use the Twelve-Step Program On The Ground one lesson at a time. If Step 5 is difficult, go back to Step 4. It's going to take time to override her mistrust.

Will this mare ever reach 100 percent of her potential? Sadly—no. She's going to need the help of a very easygoing, forgiving owner with lots of empathy for her troubled past to get to even 70 percent.

An important point here is that not everyone is cut out to work with abused or problem horses. A lot of people either don't have, or won't make, the time to rehabilitate a horse damaged by her experiences with untrustworthy humans. If you are a patient, healing person, you can find a great deal of satisfaction in helping these special horses.

Special horses need special people.

the horse that won't tie. They may choose physical abuse of the animal as a means of venting their temper, partially because the horse responds in a manner that gratifies them—they like the cringe, the flinch, and the shy.

The horse may respond in different ways to this sort of abuse. He's an essentially forgiving creature, but no horse can progress under the tutelage of an unstable person. It is like the situation of a child growing up with an alcoholic parent. Everyone walks on tiptoe so that the parent doesn't get mad and take it out on somebody.

These horses end up jumpy and nervous. They've always got one eye on you to see what you're up to. Any sudden movement on your part triggers a reaction from the horse all out of proportion. Fortunately these horses continue to put up with humans in spite of what we've done, and with patience, most of them can be salvaged.

Back to Basics

When you begin working with one of these abused cases, go back to the very first stages of training and handling. Be very slow and patient, and absolutely consistent. Keep the workouts short; perhaps do several each day (morning, afternoon, evening). Always be on the watch for an opportunity to quit on a good note, when the horse gives you the slightest indication of a positive response. He may be soft and responsive after five minutes, after ten or twenty, but you must be quick to reward that softening by stopping the work.

The quicker you can get this horse doing drills in small spaces without the use of a halter, the better. This level of work requires trust from the horse. Stay in a small area, such as a stall, a double stall, or a small pen. Moving to a large arena at this time would be too much for the frightened horse. He would be looking for an escape instead of concentrating on you. The stall is a comforting place where he is fed and watered, and he's not necessarily seeking an escape. He will be willing to let you into his space little by little and accept your control.

Be careful of how you use your eyes with this type of horse. Never let your body language express that you don't trust him. (See Chapter One to review body-language basics between horse and human, if you want a refresher.) There is no such thing as petting or rubbing this horse too much. He needs the reassurance of pleasant, confidence-building contact so that he can reconnect positively with the human race.

Let him watch and memorize your mannerisms. Move slowly around him. Giving him treats, such as carrots and grain, can start giving him the idea that you are something to focus on and not a bad person.

Rub his withers and the dock of his tail, just as his mother would have caressed him as a foal. See if you can find his favorite spot and use it often. Keep moving slowly and methodically. Work frequently for short periods until he looks forward to your arrival and comes freely over to you, entering your space. This is a big green light of progress!

Don't get in a big hurry to start normal training when you see a green light or two. Instead, go back to basics with him (see Chapter Three). Tie him out where he can see other activity and horses, particularly quiet horses. Let him get used to the activity. Start by tying him in a quiet aisle, and progress to the arena where he can watch other horses work. Go gradually, letting the horse get used to each new place. Keep to an absolute routine, and put the horse away when he appears to have responded in a positive manner.

Don't let any ruckus occur around this horse. All of your barn help should be just as quiet and consistent as you. One impatient, or rough handler can set all of your work back to square one. Take this horse through the Four Phases of RESISTANCE FREE training when he's ready and watch

him bloom with confidence. Keep in mind that under stressful conditions, he may well revert back to oversensitivity and fearful responses. That's okay—you know how to bring him back into focus. Use Patterning and the Pizza Theory anytime he's overfaced. He'll come back around more quickly each time.

There's nothing so strong as gentleness, nothing so gentle as strength.

BADLY BROUGHT UP

Some mares are naturally cranky and sournatured. They raise their foals to see the world in the same warped way in which they do. These mares sometimes end up in the broodmare band because they are so "ornery" no one wants to have to ride them. The bad-minded foals they raise can spoil the reputation of a breed or a bloodline.

The young horse grows up cranky about his space. These horses don't like to be approached by other horses, or people. They also want to stand right on top of you in your space and are quick to take a nip and get pushy.

It's important for these horses to get socialized with other horses who will educate them about their place in the pecking order. Today, when so many horses grow up isolated in small paddocks, or live with one-horse owners, they often don't get exposure to normal horse culture. The normal horse "world" operates like a little kingdom, starting with the king and going right down to the peasants. There is only one king, or one general, only one second "banana," and so forth. The solitary horse never learns these manners of horse society. He seeks to act out his dominance on the people he's exposed to, as they are all he has.

The best cure for these individuals is to turn them out with a seasoned horse, particularly an old mare or a tough gelding. My father always kept a proud-cut Shetland on the place. When we had a tough horse come in, he'd turn that horse out with the pony, and the pony would proceed to kick the daylights out of the big horse. That pony would not tolerate being picked on, and he would teach the new horse about the pecking order more efficiently than a dozen trainers could.

When one of these horses gets put in his place, he may get a little marked up, but it will make a difference like night and day when he goes back to work. He will have been taught, and now understand the idea of obedience. It doesn't hurt to rotate this horse through several different groupings. The more the merrier, reinforcing the pecking order over and over, teaching the horse that he has his place—and it's not on top of you! After this experience, it's not a difficult process to convey to him that he needs to be as subservient to you as he is to the top dog in the herd.

In training, do lots of ponying. Never work this horse without putting a chain under his chin, keeping him aware of your control without the need to give a lot of pull. Do lots of Clock Drills and other drills to make him aware of your space and presence. Avoid using the whip. Make this horse super-aware of your body movements through the drills so that he responds more freely. Workouts should be short. Afterward, leave him alone and turn him back out with the group. Let them continue the lessons you have begun.

This kind of horse can be a tough customer on the ground. He can benefit from being tied around high-traffic areas, but make sure that he can't kick anyone. You may have to put out a couple of cones to make sure that everyone gives this horse enough room when they go past.

Have the right equipment on him to make him watch and listen to you. That means a chain and a well-fitted halter. Don't be afraid to be quick and aggressive around this horse, as that is what he will respect. When the horse does give

in to you, giving a green light, rub him well, and then leave him be. Don't hang around petting and feeding him. He doesn't respect that. He can't be treated like a house pet. Think of him as a junkyard dog.

You can change this horse almost overnight if you have the right sort of pasture mates to do your training for you. This environment tells him about his proper place in the world than you ever can. Ultimately this is the kind of training that has the best results with these horses.

OVERREACTIVE HORSES

The sensitive horse often injures himself when he goes into one of his panic attacks. These horses often seem suicidal by nature, and they don't mind taking you along with them. You've seen some of these horses. They practically go over backward when you sneeze.

Reforming overreactive horses can be a difficult task. Every movement you make must be super quiet and well thought out. Do everything in slow motion and don't change the routine by so much as an inch. The routine should be consistent to the point of monotony. That will help this horse begin toning down his reactions and behaving with a normal set of responses. If possible keep him together with the quiet horses.

Some of these horses don't ever come around. Just as some people are never "right," some horses are never "right." Don't attempt to break this horse's spirit with overwork, as he can outlast you when he's operating on adrenaline and terror. When he gets his second wind, he'll hurt you when he resumes the battle you foolishly began.

This type of horse may back off a little and put you off guard. Be alert to his changing reactions and don't get careless. This type of horse benefits from coupling monotonous, slow routines with longer workouts. Start quiet and slow, and gradually increase the pressure on the horse. The more you back him, move into his space, asking him to give laterally in response to you, the better. Get into his mind and make him watch you.

Never begin work with a horse like this in a large space. Stay in a small pen until his training is well under way. A small space can be very effective for a lot of important work. Don't get impatient and go out into the open too soon. The horse will revert to earlier behaviors.

Don't ever attempt to get this horse used to frightening things by using the "flooding" technique of exposing the horse to his fears until he loses his fear. This approach will surely backfire. "Flooding" will send this horse into mental oblivion, and he'll probably hurt himself or you getting away. Don't ever tie anything to the saddle with the idea of letting him get used to it. He'll fight that frightening object until he's too badly hurt to move, or he'll run over you while you try to get control of him.

Instead, build trust and confidence. You can tie this horse out as many hours in a day as you can stand. He needs exposure to the big, bad world so that he can slowly come to realize that it isn't an awful place. Tying out teaches him patience and how to accept small pressures.

Visit this horse often and rub his nose. There's no such thing as going too slowly in his training. You have the rest of his life. Don't use a chain under his chin, or a war bridle, or any device that can create pain when he goes into one of his little panic flurries. Use a comfortable nylon, leather, or rope halter with the heavy lead rope.

In a herd situation, you can always spot this potential panicker. He's the one hanging out at the very back with twenty other horses between you and him—and he's watching you like a hawk.

Don't be disappointed with this horse. Take pride in the small increments of success you'll eventually get with him, even though he'll probably let you down on a regular basis. Just when you think you have control of his mind,

he'll come unglued at a small noise. Remember it's not your fault, it's just the way this horse is "wired." You must never punish him for his freak-outs. If you lose your temper, it's like a snowball rolling downhill reinforcing his fear and giving him darn good reason to panic.

Use your voice a lot, sticking to steady, chant-like tones that help the horse start relaxing. Remember that this horse can do something silly or stupid at the drop of a hat, so always be ready. Don't sell this animal to someone who isn't experienced enough to deal with him, and particularly don't let someone with a short fuse get his hands on him. You'll need the patience of a saint to make something out of him—you'll put many more hours in than on a whole herd of normal horses. Just make sure that he's worth all that time and patience.

SPOILED ROTTEN?

The spoiled pet is typically an orphan, hand-raised, or often the single horse of a backyard owner who has doted on the animal since birth. What's cute and charming in a two-week-old colt becomes dangerous when the animal tops 1000 pounds and has no manners or restraint.

This horse is always in your space and challenging you. If you don't give him the carrot, he nips at your fingers. The horse learned this behavior because no one ever told him "no." With an orphan foal, it often begins with bottle-feeding, when he's allowed to get cranky because the bottle is late, or not filling enough.

He always wants to do the opposite of what he's told. If you want him to stand, he'll squirrel around. If you want him to move, you won't be able to dislodge him from his tracks. Don't go after him with a whip and a chain. Begin by tying him in his stall, where he can't get hurt. Put a nylon halter and sturdy cotton rope on him and let him pull back as much as he likes. Make sure that there are no buckets or anything in the stall that can cause injury. Let him have his tantrums, but keep an eye on him.

When he's quiet about being tied in his stall, move him to a corral or an aisle with a little traffic. He won't want to stand still initially, but he'll learn over the span of a couple of hours.

In about the third week of this kind of work, I start tying him in the arena, letting him relax and be quiet. He can see the other horses, but he has to stand. Use a chain under his chin so that you have the advantage in the training, but do not tie him with the chain on.

By keeping the advantage at all times, you'll find that training goes relatively quickly once the initial learning has soaked in. He learns patience from the tying, and the halter and chain under his chin give you a mechanical advantage over him. Be firm and make him learn to yield and give to you.

Help this horse learn to focus and yield by working him intensely once a day and then leave him alone. Don't keep pecking at him, and don't repeat a lesson over and over. Do it just as much as it takes to get him to respond, then go on to something else.

Like the thief in the night seeking an open door, look for the opportunity to quit on a positive note. When he respects and watches you and works quietly, rub on him and put him away. When he hits you with his head or pushes into you, get tough right back at him. Make him respect you by using quick body movements which explain that he is firmly below you in the pecking order.

Don't start working this horse when you are short of time. You can't finish a session until he gives, and that might be an hour. If you can't give him all the time he needs, don't start. If you have to give up before he gives in, you reinforce the old problem behavior. When you do see a soft response, don't do another thing. The next time it will take a little less time to get to that point, but you always have to be ready for that day when he gets up on the wrong side of the stall and wants to be a tough guy.

CASE STUDY: SECRETARIATE IMPRESSION

Secretariate Impression is a two-year-old filly who hasn't been handled much. She's spent most of her time in a pasture by herself, growing up. In the stable and around other horses, she is nervous and seems to spook at everything. She trusts no one. Her owners are afraid that someday she is going to seriously hurt herself when she panics.

Her Thoroughbred breeding contributes to her sensitivity. Add in the fact that she hasn't been socialized around other horses, and her lack of confidence makes a lot of sense.

With this type of horse, you can never spend too much time grooming. Keep everything slow. Do all drills and exercises, and move around her in slow motion.

It's important to remember that when she spooks, she's really frightened. It's nothing personal. Take a deep breath, talk to her slowly in a low voice, and try to keep a hand on her for reassurance. In her early training, work in a stall or other small area as much as possible. Look for quiet green lights before you end a session.

Turn her out for exercise with quiet, older horses at least twice a week. Spend twice as long ponying her to get her used to traffic and other horses. Really sensitive horses should spend a lot of time at the walk and trot. Plan on not going faster than a trot for the first 90 days of work. When riding, rub her neck and rump frequently. And you can never do too many circles. Keep the routines predictable and your requests stress-free and always reward green lights.

Horses like Secretariate Impression will teach you patience.

THE IMPORTANCE OF PREDICTABILITY

Recognize all these types of difficult horses and learn everything you can about what makes them tick. Speak to their owners or handlers and watch them in the corral and around the barn as they interact with other horses and people. There is no such thing as a bad horse, though some are a little better than others.

In my whole life, I've never seen a horse I couldn't improve a little bit. However, you can't necessarily produce a world champion when you are working with flawed horses like these. You can make him a better citizen of the world, and that is enough.

It's your job as a trainer to establish a positive routine that gives the horse everything he needs and lets him know what to expect. Feed at the same time, clean stalls at the same time, and bring him in at the same time. Do the same warm-up, the same drills, and the same schooling techniques that build on the horse's knowledge in a progressive manner. Consistency makes the horse better prepared to accept the new learning.

In the wild, the horse does everything in a fairly set routine. He gets his drink at the same time each day, sleeps in the same area each day, and moves about on a similar schedule each day. If you feed the domestic horse at a set time each day, he will learn to anticipate that and be waiting. The horse has a clock in his head. Don't be an unpredictable trainer. Routine is essential. If you don't adopt a routine, you won't create a reliable learning process.

Knowing when to quit is especially important when training challenging horses. I've seen trainers who work one-third of the time everyone else does with twice the success. They always know when to stop, when to repeat, and how to make use of a routine that takes the pressure off the horse. They've mastered the art of learning to "read" the horse. As soon as he licks, chews, takes a deep breath, and relaxes his body, it's time to go to something else.

When the problem horse has the basics under his cinch, begin him right at the beginning of the Four Phases of RESISTANCE FREE training, even if he's been a saddle horse for years. Go back to the basics to repattern this horse's old habits. Remember that groundwork produces steadiness and teaches the troubled horse about consistency. As I've said before, you can't do too much groundwork. Use his natural instincts and teach him to keep moving until you give permission to stop. This underlines the fact that you are above him in the pecking order. Listen to the horse and advance training when he tells you he's ready.

Rehabilitating challenging horses will test your knowledge and your character, but the rewards are priceless. Turn problems into challenges and use exercises to solve problems. Give the horse the chance to be obedient. And take heart in knowing that horses' attitudes can be changed with communication, patience, and RESISTANCE FREE training.

---

*Remember, horses don't have goals—
people do.*

Is a Career in Training in Your Future?

Know yourself. Are you a really social person who needs other human beings in order to flourish? Horse training is a very solitary activity. Even when you're riding in the same arena with a large group of people, you are still concentrating on you and your horse. If you are dependent on the feedback and companionship of other people, training horses isn't necessarily right for you.

Research your chosen field as much as possible. Learn about breeding and which bloodlines are successful at which events. Learn all of the "ins" and "outs" of your preferred events and what it takes to come out of the ring as a winner. Learn the skills that are required for good horse management. You will need to be able to feed, groom, and exercise the horse (or horses) in an appropriate manner to enhance performance development. There's a lot more to it than turning him out in a field and bringing him in once a day.

The horses you make will reflect your personality. Are you happy with what you see in your reflection? Evaluate yourself on a balance sheet. List your strengths and liabilities. Remember that this should be a business-like evaluation, and you must have more assets than liabilities if you intend to build a thriving business.

Sending a horse out into the world is like throwing a pebble into a pond. The ripples keep spreading out and touching more and more people. A good horse can impact dozens of people in a favorable way, sometimes more. If you do good, professional work, you can be proud to say you were a part of that horse's beginning. If the idea of seeing a horse fulfill his promise over a lifetime gives you satisfaction, then this career might suit you just fine.

One of my biggest thrills came when I was judging at the Kansas City Royal one year and saw a little freckle-faced girl in the eleven-and-under pleasure class who was getting a real "Cadillac ride" from her horse. She won the class going away, and when the class was announced, I got goose bumps. The horse was one I had started long, long ago. Several students had shown him before he was sold, and here he was again, still a teacher and companion in his twenties.

Working with horses is a privilege that is not available to everyone. Don't take it lightly. The responsibility is immense, not only for you and the horse right now, but for both your futures. It takes time, skill, and hard work. You can't do it once or twice a month and get anywhere. But when you've done it right and created the harmony that results in a horse that can change leads, turn a cow, or thread his way through a complex trail obstacle, you can be proud.

The mediocre horse trainer tells.

The good horse trainer explains.

The superior horse trainer demonstrates.

The great horse trainer inspires.

Above the Bit

The horse is in an inverted frame with his head held higher than the withers. The neck is commonly ewe-shaped in horses that are poorly built or have been badly ridden for a long period of time. The front line of the face is typically pointed outward, rather than vertical, and in extreme cases, the horse may resemble an alligator, with his head held horizontally. The horse's back will be hollow, typically with the hocks trailing out behind the body. The withers are not "up," but instead are dropped, and the rider is astride a drooping suspension bridge. Horses in this posture are typically tense and respond to cues by further hollowing themselves.

Behind the Bit

Horses who are behind the bit are typically curving their neck at the third vertebra instead of the first vertebra immediately behind the poll. The front line of the face is not vertical, but tilted inward, toward the horse's chest. Contact with the bit is often minimal, as these horses coil themselves into a posture that comes right up to the bit without taking an honest contact. This fault can be more difficult to correct than being **above the bit** because it is more subtle. The inexperienced rider is often fooled into thinking that it is correct because the horse is curved and appears willing. Horses who are behind the bit are not using their hindquarters effectively. This fault is extremely common in horses that have been forced into position by the use of draw reins.

Bosal

This is a shaped noseband of braided leather used in the early training of the horse. Green horses are started in thick bosals, and the thickness of the bosal is gradually reduced as the horse progresses in his education. There are no metal parts on a true bosal at all. The bosal works by applying pressure to the poll, the bridge of the nose, and the chin.

Bubble

This refers to the horse's personal space over which he feels dominant. Some horses greatly resent an intrusion into their "bubble," or space; others welcome it. You have a "bubble" as well—at what point do you feel uncomfortable at the nearness of strangers? You may resent the individual who insists on standing almost on top of you in a nearly-empty elevator!

Cadence

Refers to the rhythm of the footfalls, when rhythm is accented with elasticity of movement. The horse moves with activity, yet precisely and correctly, in perfect rhythm. A good horse can become a brilliant horse with the addition of cadence to his performance. It can be difficult to explain cadence but it is easy to recognize it. These horses draw your eye to their excellence.

Center/Centered

Your center is located just above and within the cage of your pelvis. It is the location of your **center of gravity** and the "heart" of your body as far as physical activity is concerned. Do not confuse your center with your belly button. If you went inward several inches from your bellybutton to the central core of your body, you would be at your center.

Center of Gravity

A dynamic point that is always changing with the motion of the horse or person. It is the point of balance, which shifts according to momentum and posture. When you are standing, your **center** and your center of gravity coincide. When you are sprinting in the 100-yard dash, your center of gravity is moving forward and upward into your trunk to a point where all forces are in balance. If your center of gravity gets too far forward, you will fall on your face.

Cow/Cowhorse

The quality shown by a horse that expresses an interest in working or playing with cattle. Actually a horse with "cow" will work anything, from children to chickens, as it is an instinctive response to movement. In the top horses, "cow" is also shown in the ability to read an animal and anticipate which way it will move next.

Curb Bit

A bit with leverage that applies pressure on the poll, the chin groove, and the bars of the mouth. Any bit that does not have a direct line of connection between your hand and the bit is typically a curb bit. The length and ratio of the shanks determine the severity of a curb bit. A curb bit can be loose-jaw with hinged shanks that move, or rigid, as in the grazing-type bits that do not have any points of movement in the bit itself. There are many different mouthpieces available in curb bits for all different horse sports.

Dressage

Means training. It also refers to a popular horse sport that is one of the three classical sports, the other two being show jumping and three-day eventing. Dressage is based on the classical methods of horse training that date back to the ancient Greeks who first used it to prepare their cavalry horses.

Green Lights

See **Red and Green Lights**

Hard Eyes

A rider with hard, narrow eyes has a fixed focus on one point, often the horse's ears, and can be stiff and quite unaware of the surroundings.

Hunt Seat

A style of horsemanship derived from the cavalry methods, oriented toward riding on the flat and jumping. It is one of three types of English riding. The rider is more forward with his upper body in order to follow the horse's **center of gravity** while jumping and riding fast cross-country.

In the Bridle

A horse that is in the bridle is actively engaged behind and carries his back and withers in an upward posture, like a suspension bridge that slightly arches up, to carry the rider efficiently. The head is vertical, and the horse carries the bit with the appropriate contact for the style of riding and the type of bit. His movement is elastic and lively, with a true cadence and springiness that makes him light and pleasurable to watch. He is immediately alert for any maneuver through the use of **Preparatory Commands** and is totally without resistance throughout his body and mind.

On the Bit

A horse that is on the bit is in an active and lively posture, which enables him to perform any maneuver if he is given the appropriate **Preparatory Commands**. It differs from **in the bridle** in that the horse may be in a more upright posture, with a more raised head and neck, but continuing to show a correct shape and arch of the neck. The back and withers are carried in an arch rather than a sag, and the horse is carrying more of his weight on his hind legs than on his front legs. He is well engaged behind in order to support more of his body weight on the hind legs, making his forehand more mobile and light.

Patterning

A step further than imprinting. I came up with this term about ten years ago. It consists of turning a negative into a positive. For example, if we're going to get a horse used to a saddle blanket, I approach the horse with the blanket, with my eyes down and my body in a non-threatening posture. As soon as the horse begins to show resistance or panic, I stop, turn my back and walk away. After a moment or two, I walk back up to him. I may get a foot closer before he begins to show me **red lights**. Eventually he accepts it, looks at it, and bonds with it.

Pecking Order

Animals and birds sort out a hierarchy within their groups that determines who is in charge and who has dominance over another. There will be a General, or the leader, and there will be the Private, the one who is at the very bottom of the ranks. In training horses, we usually want a horse out of the middle of the pack for best results.

Pizza Theory

Refers to the practice of doing an exercise a little bit at a time, in tiny bites that are easy for the horse to "swallow." You break down a problem or a new idea into the smallest possible increments and teach the horse each little step before moving on to the next.

Preparatory Commands

Subtle warning cues that instruct the horse to adjust his balance and position in order to be ready for an action or transition.

Red and Green Lights

These are important messages from your horse. "Red lights" indicate resistance. They may look like confusion, tension, disobedience, or panic. Sometimes resistance looks like shutting down, the horse just tunes you out as if you were invisible. "Green lights" are the go-ahead signs that indicate that learning is possible. When the horse drops his head, licks and chews, takes a breath, yawns, and is otherwise relaxed and interested, his mind and heart are receptive to you and the lessons you present. The horse can't learn unless his green lights are glowing.

Resistance Free Horsemanship

The result of a horse and rider working in complete harmony and unity, with no resistance in the body or mind of either. It is our goal, no matter what horse sport we perform.

Rhythm

Refers to the sequence and consistency of the footfalls of the horse. For example, a horse who is four-beating at the canter is showing impure rhythm. It would be impossible for a four-beater to show **cadence**. A limping horse is also unable to show correct rhythm or cadence.

Saddle Seat

A style of horsemanship designed to showcase gaited breeds such as the American Saddlebred and the Tennessee Walker and also a popular style for breeds such as the Morgan, Arabian, and, occasionally, the Appaloosa.

Security Deposits

I often compare using positive reinforcement and the other Resistance Free training principles to making deposits into a training "bank account." If you make more security deposits—soothing rubs on the withers, or timely uses of the **Pizza Theory**, for instance—than withdrawals—such as meeting resistance with resistance or, worse, temper—your account stays in the black. Keep this account "in the black" with regular investments of positive reinforcement. The result will be a secure and confident horse.

Snaffle Bit

A bit that does not have leverage. It influences the horse strictly through pressure on the lips and tongue. It can be a tool of finesse or a means of cruelty in the wrong hands.

Soft Eyes

A rider with soft, open eyes shows complete and total awareness of his surroundings and the activities going on therein. When using open eyes, the rider automatically places himself in a more relaxed and correct posture to always look to his destination, the horizon.

Stock Seat

The formal term for Western horsemanship. It derives its name from originally being the practical and comfortable horsemanship of the cowboy and vaquero.

Sweet Spot

The place in the saddle where you are naturally inclined to sit. In a well-designed saddle, this will be in a place that encourages and allows good riding position. In poorly designed saddles, the sweet spot may be placed in such a manner as to encourage you to sit out of balance and make it impossible for you to go with the movement of the horse.

Tempo

The rate of striding or footfalls. It does not necessarily relate to speed. A horse can have a fast tempo but still be taking short strides, as is seen in the racking Saddlebred. The Western horse typically has a relaxed tempo with good length of stride.

Transition

The act of changing from one gait or movement to the next. It can be done roughly without warning, or it can be a smooth, Resistance Free action that flows without interruption.

RESISTANCE FREE RESOURCES

The training tools from Richard Shrake listed below (as well as other resources), are available from:

A Winning Way, Ltd.
P.O. Box 4490
Sunriver, OR 97707

Telephone: (800) 635-8861
Fax: (541) 593-5811
www.richardshrake.com

THE RHYTHM COLLECTOR

This simple tool teaches the horse to permanently relax his poll, move his forehand and hindquarters in balance, and develop his muscles for maximum collection. An instructional video with step-by-step instructions on how to use The Rhythm Collector is included.

THE CONNECTOR® BIT

A transition bit to help the horse progress from a snaffle to a curb bit. The three-part mouthpiece gives a pre-signal to the horse's tongue, lips, and mouth corners. The rein attachment is curved back and gives a slow, mild signal.

VIDEO SERIES

The Resistance Free Video Series covers topics such as:
The Problem Horse
Showmanship/Halter
Resistance Free Riding
Horse Psychology & Groundwork
Masters Series Horsemanship
Trail
Bits & Bitting
and many more.

BOOKS

Western Horsemanship by Richard Shrake
Topics range from selecting a horse, exercises, transitions, psychology, and riding tips.

Resistance Free Riding by Richard Shrake
Add Resistance Free riding techniques such as soft eyes, correct breathing, Preparatory Commands, the ripple effect, and positive mental preparation to your horsemanship skills across all riding disciplines, and enhance your effectiveness in the saddle.

Richard Shrake also offers Graduate, Master, and Apprentice programs, riding programs, and clinics across the United States. Contact **A Winning Way, Ltd.,** for further information.

Page numbers in *italic* indicate photographs.